MANAGING CONSULTANTS

MANAGING WORK AND ORGANIZATIONS SERIES

Edited by Graeme Salaman, Reader in Sociology in the Faculty of Social Sciences and the Open Business School, the Open University

Current and forthcoming titles include:

MANAGING CONSULTANTS
CONSULTANCY AS THE
MANAGEMENT OF IMPRESSIONS

Timothy Clark

Open University Press
Buckingham · Philadelphia

Open University Press
Celtic Court
22 Ballmoor
Buckingham
MK18 1XW

and
1900 Frost Road, Suite 101
Bristol, PA 19007, USA

First Published 1995

A catalogue record of this book is available from the British Library

ISBN   0 335 19219 X (pb)   0 335 19220 3 (hb)

Library of Congress Cataloging-in-Publication Data
Clark, Timothy, 1964–
    Managing consultants: consultancy as the management of
impressions/Timothy Clark.
        p.   cm. – (Managing work and organizations)
    Includes bibliographical references and index.
    ISBN 0-335-19220-3 (hb). – ISBN 0-335-19219-X (pb)
    1. Business consultants – Great Britain.   2. Management – Great
Britain.   3. Business consultants.   4. Management.   I. Title.
II. Series: Managing work and organizations series.
HD69.C6C533   1995
001—dc20   95-15675
                                                                    CIP

Typeset by Type Study, Scarborough
Printed in Great Britain by St Edmundsbury Press Ltd,
Bury St Edmunds, Suffolk

CONTENTS

This book is dedicated to the memory of Jeremy Schoeffer –
a fellow traveller and more often than not my guide

LIST OF TABLES AND FIGURES

Tables

Figures

ACKNOWLEDGEMENTS

This book represents perhaps the final stopover on a research journey which began at Leicester Business School, de Montfort University. I am indebted to Derrick Ball, Stephen Batstone, Ian Beardwell, Christine Britton, Ian Clark and Clive Harrison for their unswerving support and encouragement during the initial phases of the research. I am grateful for the many discussions I have had with Geoff Mallory and Derek Pugh at the School of Management, The Open University, which have greatly influenced the development of my recent thinking. I would also like to offer my sincere thanks to Estelle Moon and Mina Panchal for their assistance with the preparation of certain parts of the manuscript. My special thanks go to Graeme Salaman, without whose active and constructive support the book may never have come about. Finally, I would like to thank the numerous consultants and users of consultancy services who gave their hard pressed time so generously and contributed to my understanding of the management consultancy industry.

1

INTRODUCTION

Organizations of all kinds are increasingly turning to management consultancies for assistance with a wide range of management issues and problems. Indeed, during the latter part of the 1980s the management consultancy industry was one of the fastest growing sectors of the UK economy. For instance, between 1985 and 1992 the industry expanded by a little over 200 per cent (Business Statistics Office, 1985, 1992). In contrast, over the same period the manufacturing sector grew by 6 per cent, the service sector as a whole grew by a little under 30 per cent and the business service sector expanded by 80 per cent. These figures indicate that the shift in the axis of the British economy away from the manufacturing sector to the service sector continued apace into the 1980s. However, this trend does not simply equate with an absolute reduction of the manufacturing sector and an equivalent expansion of the service sector. Rather, current trends are more accurately characterized as a process of industrial restructuring in which particular service industries, primarily business services, have moved to take up a more central position in the British economy. Management consultancy has been one of the most dynamic industries in this increasingly significant and vibrant sector of the British economy.

There are two interrelated reasons for this increase in the use of management consultancies. First, organizations, in response to what are perceived to be radical changes and increased pressures from their markets and competitors, are increasingly likely to have embarked, or likely to be embarking, on programmes of profound organizational change. Second, by virtue of the nature of this actual or planned organizational change, managers are likely to believe that new skills, values and qualities are necessary; these are currently lacking. Essentially, therefore, from all sides managers are being convinced, or at least persuaded, that traditional structures, systems and cultures will no longer do; that the organization must change fundamentally. It must change paradigms and the designing and managing of this change, and working in the changed organization, will require new skills.

Hence, the increasing use of management consultancies is linked to the current pressures for change facing most, if not all, organizations. In the past organizational environments were classified on a continuum ranging from stable at one extreme to turbulent at the other. Within a stable unpressured environment the need for consultants is significantly reduced. Why would they be necessary when there is nothing to change? But, in fact, there never have been completely stable environments, just environments that were perceived as static, where organizations failed to detect the small signs of emerging threat and change. Alternatively, organizations reacted to their environments in terms of established ways of doing things, which, since they had always worked, required no change or replacement. But now change is recognized as necessary. This is evidenced by a survey conducted in the mid-1980s, which reported that a third of senior executives polled claimed that their organizations were undergoing *radical* strategic change (Thomson *et al.*, 1985). Today the proportion would probably be higher. For instance, Storey and Sisson (1993) report that in a study of 15 UK organizations two-thirds reported change on 11 out of 25 key dimensions of human resource management (HRM). They note that 'Such has been the apparent level of engagement with these new sets of beliefs, values and practices that the evidence points to a wholesale shift away from the proceduralist recipe in our major employing organization' (p. 19). By 'proceduralist' these authors mean management by recipe – by reference to established, time-honoured and formalized procedures and rules. Their research results suggest that established habits and methods of management are now seen as insufficient, even as positively unhelpful. The emphasis now is on reducing constraints and controls in order to 'liberate' the capacities of the individual and to encourage initiative and enterprise.

Coulson-Thomas (1991: 3), summarizing the results from a number of surveys into the changing nature of organizations writes 'Organizations face an unprecedented range of challenges and opportunities in the social, economic, political and business environment. This external environment is characterized by uncertainty, surprise, turbulence and discontinuity'. He points out that the survey evidence suggests the following trends:

- to survive in the face of multiple challenges organizations are having to become more flexible and responsive;
- work is increasingly being delegated to multifunctional, multi-location and multinational teams, and assessment is switching from input to output;
- organization structures are becoming flatter and more fluid, and developing into networks, with computerized links to customers, suppliers and business partners;
- there is an increasing requirement for a 'new approach to management', with more responsibility being 'pushed down' to middle managers who require flexible access to expertise and specialists.

Thus, a consensus is beginning to emerge among many management commentators, which suggests that for most organizations the traditional dichotomy between stable and turbulent environments is no longer relevant. Instead, for the majority of organizations environments have become increasingly uncertain, turbulent and unpredictable. In response to these changed, and constantly changing, circumstances, organizations are having to embark on programmes of radical change; they are having to reinvent themselves. In Buchanan and Boddy's (1992: 41) terms managers are increasingly 'managing in quadrant four'. This is the most problematic situation in which to manage organizational change, since the changes demanded strike at the organization's core activity and are *'seen as a radical departure from existing arrangements'* (emphasis added, p. 42). Salaman (1995) has traced the key pressures that have underpinned recent organizational transformations. The following discussion draws on his detailed analysis.

According to a study sponsored by the Foundation for Management Education and Ashridge Management College (Ashridge Management Research Group, 1987) the organization of the future 'will form a different context for the practice of management. A context within which flexibility and commitment will be key attributes within the decentralized but strongly integrated organization' (p. 37). This is echoed by Beer *et al.* 1988, 1990), who argue that the key to organizational success is to change the way managers work. They argue that in order to re-establish their dominance, regain market share or ensure continued survival, many organizations 'are reducing reliance on managerial authority, formal rules and procedures, and narrow divisions of work. And they are creating teams, sharing information, and delegating responsibility and accountability far down the hierarchy' (p. 158).

There is evidence that decentralization is occurring and is beneficial. Pettigrew and Whipp (1991), for example, on the basis of a study of market leaders in a number of sectors of UK industry, identify five variables that account for high performance: capacity to assess the external environment, leading change, linking strategic and operational change, regarding human resources as assets and coherence in the management of change. Furthermore, they write:

> The ability of a company to learn should be under constant scrutiny. In other words, the ability of the organization to reconstruct and adapt its knowledge base (made up of skills, structures and values) should be a key task for managers. They should also be able to apply the 'unlearning' test. In other words, is the organization capable of mounting the creative destruction necessary to break down outmoded attitudes and practices, while at the same time building up new, more appropriate competence? (Pettigrew and Whipp, 1991: 290)

As firms diversify, according to Goold and Campbell (1987: 1), 'they move away from being functionally organized towards a divisional structure, in which responsibility is pushed down to business units and profit centre managers'. Hill and Pickering (1986), in a study of 144 large UK companies, found that nearly all of them had moved or were moving towards greater decentralization. It has been noted that the reasons for the move towards decentralization are complex and involve an interplay between corporate and HR strategies (Purcell and Ahlstrand, 1994). It has also been noted that the outcome of the process can vary, producing different types of decentralized organization (Goold and Campbell, 1987). But the point being developed here is that the empirical pervasiveness of fundamental structural change is likely to stimulate concern among managers, not only with the design and management of the changes themselves, but also with the identification, assessment and development of the new managerial qualities necessary within the new structures.

As noted above, the prevalence of change is one issue; the type of change occurring, or recommended, is another. Managers, as they face increased competitive pressure resulting from deregulation, reduced product life cycles, differentiated markets, globalization and so forth, are exposed to the siren voices of management commentators and consultants telling them how they must change radically to meet these new demands. It is not simply that, as Makridakis (1992: 12) argues, in future competitive advantage 'will be gained by developing/introducing new products . . . and/or by creating new needs. Thus, identifying new markets and creating new wants, and introducing new fads and fashions will become imperative'. In addition, future competitive success will require new forms of organization, new attitudes and new behaviours. So there is not simply a need to change from structure A to structure B but to a situation of constant change and responsiveness where even the ways of changing are changing. In other words, managers are being asked, even commanded, to take a leap in the dark; to move from an established and familiar way of doing things to a way of working whose main property is its strangeness, fluidity and evanescence.

The new type of organization, we are advised, is characterized by its inherent and unlimited flexibility, its capacity to learn and develop. 'The most successful corporation of the 1990s will be something called a learning organization, a consummately adaptive organization' (Dumaine, 1989: 24). Definitions of this form of organization abound (see, for example, Pedler *et al.*, 1986; Megginson and Pedler, 1992; Mills and Friesen 1992), but the detail is not relevant to this discussion. What are of importance are the implications of this essentially metaphoric way of conceptualizing organization structure and process for management and management attributes. Sashkin and Burke (1990) emphasize the importance of leaders who can develop these organizations but sadly note that most managers are not qualified for the task. As Senge (1990: 22) writes, 'it should come as no surprise that such organizations will remain a distant vision until the leadership capabilities they demand are developed'. Thus, 'the 1990s may be the period during which organizational development and (a new sort of) management development are reconnected' (Sashkin and Burke, 1990; quoted in Senge, 1990: 22).

What management qualities are required? The list is daunting. Morgan (1992: 24), for example, highlights three qualities: (a) the development of *proactive mind sets*; (b) the ability to manage *from the outside in*; and (c) the development of *positioning and repositioning skills* (these refer to the importance of sensing the environment, identifying opportunities, seeing the environment from the outside instead of in terms of established organizational categories and assumptions). Makridakis (1992: 15–16) argues that 'Top managers. . .will be rare and paradoxical: creative and practical, visionary and pragmatic, flexible and persistent, easygoing and demanding, risk-taking and conservative.' In a similar vein Schroder (1989) has identified 11 'high performance managerial competencies'. These are: information search, concept formation, conceptual flexibility, interpersonal search, managing interaction, development orientation, impact, self-confidence, presentation, proactive orientation and achievement orientation.

A frequent element of most of the analyses of the managerial qualities necessary to build and work within the new learning organization is the capacity to transcend the assumptions and recipes of the past. The role of the manager/leader is to surface, confront and move beyond the tacit assumptions and paradigms of organizational processes, roles and structures. Leaders in learning organizations, argues Senge (1990: 12), are responsible for restructuring the reality for their staff so that they 'see beyond the superficial conditions and events into the underlying causes of problems' and therefore 'see new possibilities for shaping the future'.

In a similar fashion Drucker (1988) argues that the main challenge for managers in the 1990s is not whatever may change in their turbulent business environment but ensuring that tomorrow's challenges are not handled with yesterday's logic. The problem for managers is that organizations encourage and then institutionalize in culture and routines particular ways of thinking (i.e. mind sets). These are the organization's success recipes; their formulas for continued success. When required to act or decide the manager, like all of us, will have recourse to a stock of recipes. These are the rules and skills that arise out of a manager's vocational life and practical experience. This process can be so speedy, so skilful, that it invariably occurs subconsciously or instinctively. As a consequence, managers fail to question the relevance and appropriateness of these recipes; they fail the 'unlearning' test referred to earlier. This makes it all the more dangerous, for sooner or later these institutionalized organizational success recipes can become failure recipes. The danger is all the greater if the manager or organization does not realize the inappropriateness of the response. Indeed, the dangers are worse than this since embedded recipes can actually distort or disguise the primary data available, as numerous historical examples demonstrate: for example, Stalin's conviction that the Germans would not invade the Soviet Union after the German–Soviet non-aggression pact of 1939 led him to ignore as irrelevant and unworrying the numerous warnings from Soviet intelligence that the attack was imminent. Thus, the risk is that available and relevant data may not be noticed or may be seen as relevant but be misunderstood. In each case, the capacity of the organization to act as a learning organization is critical. As Drucker (1988) has noted (and this could be the epitaph for the organizations that fail) that the greatest danger in times of turbulence is not the turbulence but to meet the challenges of the future with yester-day's solutions and logic.

The implications of this analysis are considerable. As Kanter (1989: 89) writes,

> Managerial work is undergoing such enormous and rapid change that many managers are reinventing their profession as they go. With little precedent to guide them, they are watching hierarchy fade away and the clear distinctions of title, task, department, even corporation, blur.

This puts an enormous burden on managers. If the rule book is to be thrown out, if hierarchy is no longer the key, then organiz-ations and management will have to be reinvented. This will need help from the outside, for very clearly the people who recognize the need to change will themselves be part of what needs to be changed and will therefore be in an unfavourable position to think about and design, let alone implement, what needs to be done. Furthermore, they are told that they must lose old ways, recipes and mental sets and develop new skills, habits and insight. Yet, as we know from writers such as Mintzberg (1980), managers actually spend their time on much more humdrum activities. They are overburdened with work and as a result of work pressures are driven to 'brevity, fragmentation, and superficiality' in their work tasks. Yet they find delegation – which might offer some assistance – difficult. Moreover, the manager is encouraged to attend to the current, the here-and-now, to immerse him or herself in busyness, activity, the tangible, rather than to spend time in reflection, planning and unlearning the old and in questioning the recipes and mind sets that have served well enough in the past (Mintzberg, 1980: 173).

These points are echoed by Hales (1986) who, on the basis of a comprehensive review of research into the question 'What do managers do?', writes 'Much of what managers do is, of necessity, an unreflective response to circumstances. The man-ager is less a slow and methodical decision maker, more a "doer" who has to react rapidly to problems as they arise, "think on his feet", take decisions *in situ* and develop a preference for concrete activities' (Hales, 1986: 102). It is therefore hardly surprising that, as Dale (1994: 30) has noted, 'it is not uncommon to hear senior managers say that they feel powerless to achieve change, and that their opportunities to develop are limited.'

It is in the context of these pressures and demands that managers feel it necessary to seek increasing external support by turning to those who offer some solution to these dilemmas – the management consultants. This is confirmed by the recent expansion of the management consultancy industry mentioned at the beginning of this chapter. It would therefore appear that while these conditions persist and intensify, as many commentators predict, the continued growth and prosperity of the management consultancy industry is assured. According to this scenario management consultancies will become an increasingly significant feature of organizational life. This may be manifested in a number of different ways and not simply restricted to one-off assignments. For example, organizations are increasingly externalizing (i.e. outsourcing) the running of key services to management consultancies. In the public sector this is a process that has been given momentum by the government policy of compulsory competitive tendering (CCT). As a result of this policy management consultancies are increasingly providing *and* managing information technology (IT) services on behalf of central government departments, local authorities and National Health Service (NHS) bodies. Another trend is the employment of consultants for longer and longer periods of time, so that the line between external, impartial, advisor and substitute management becomes blurred. Perhaps the most publicized case of this is the employment of Mr Oliver Roux, a partner of Bain & Company, on the board of Guinness as director of financial strategy. However, this is no longer an isolated case. A greater number of consultants are finding themselves as semi-permanent members of their clients' senior management teams. Given the previous discussion their advice is constantly being sought by managers who feel overrun by events, unable to respond to external pressures in a reflective, considered and planned manner, and so incapable of identifying and developing the managerial qualities necessary to build an organization that will prosper in markets that are altering radically – for this they require external assistance.

An important, and much overlooked, implication of this growth in the management consultancy industry is the increase in the number of selection decisions being made. As organizations increasingly turn to management consultancies for external support and assistance they are having, many for the first time, to identify and select the consultancy they feel is most appropriate for their particular needs. The importance of making the right choice should not be underestimated, since consultancy services are not cheap and mistakes can be difficult, if not impossible, to rectify. Large consultancy projects can run for several years, with the final costs rising to many millions of pounds. Even smaller, short-term, projects can cost tens of thousands of pounds. But, perhaps more importantly, the effects of consultancy interventions are often long-term and difficult, if not impossible, to reverse. A consultancy may recommend the implementation of a particular strategy, which involves a focus on certain products and markets with the consequent disposal of a number of peripheral businesses. If this new strategy should subsequently fail, the impact on the organization may be enormous and even terminal. The formulation and implementation of an alternative strategy will take time, during which the organization may lose its position in the market place.

Furthermore, it was argued above that managers are increasingly seeking assistance from management consultancies with the design and implementation of programmes of organizational change. Essentially, it was suggested that managers seek external support because they are often powerless to effect the necessary organizational change themselves. They are part of what needs changing and the nature of the management task makes it difficult for managers to think reflectively so that they might develop and institute programmes of planned organizational change. This is made more difficult by the fact that managers tend to focus on current, here-and-now problems, giving little attention and priority to the long-term future direction of the organization. As a consequence, when managers employ consultancies they are very dependent upon them to make up for these shortcomings. In addition, in many change programmes the 'hassle factor is likely to be high. Time-scales and budgets are likely to be critical. The changes are likely to involve irreversible long-term commitments. The penalties for error will therefore be high. The personal vulnerability of the change agent is thus likely to be correspondingly high' (Buchanan and Boddy, 1992: 42). The purchase of management consultancy services is therefore often accompanied by high levels of expectation on the part of clients. For these reasons the initial selection of a management consultancy is vital. Clients must attempt to select consultancies that will provide the services they require and meet their level of expectations. If they make a wrong choice at the outset, the long-term consequences for the organization could be disastrous.

However, a number of commentators have argued that there are inherent problems associated with the use of management consultancies (Holmstrom, 1985; Clark, 1993b; Mitchell, 1994). Two main problems are commonly identified. The first relates to the difficulties potential purchasers have in determining the precise nature of a consultancy's service prior to purchase. What is it that is being offered and how does this compare to other consultancies? The second problem concerns the difficulties in establishing whether the consultancy did a good job. Did the consultancy do what it was asked to do? Clients want to be assured that they received the service they paid for. At the same time they are seeking confirmation that their initial selection decision was the correct one. There is nothing more disappointing, from the client's viewpoint, than to discover that he or she made the wrong choice; this just compounds problems when selecting a consultancy in the future. Furthermore, clients are looking for evidence that can be used to inform future selection decisions. Can I, or should I, use the same consultancy again?

The decision as to which consultancy a client chooses to use for a particular assignment depends crucially on the availability and accuracy of information about the service a supplier offers and the client's assessment of this at the pre-purchase stage. This information enables clients to evaluate the quality of the alternatives they may be considering. Information that may be of use to clients when choosing a consultancy might include some evidence that the consultancy understands the problems the client faces, an estimate of the length of the assignment, biographies of relevant consultancy staff, examples of similar assignments undertaken by the consultancy as well as some indication of the expected cost. However, a number of characteristics of consultancy services imply that the quality of a service is difficult for clients to verify prior to purchase. Specifically, services have a number of unique features that distinguish them from goods. At the pre-purchase stage these characteristics can severely restrict the availability, and distort the accuracy, of relevant information, making the purchase decision problematic. These difficulties are perhaps best illustrated with reference to a particular example.

Consider the purchase of a haircut. We are looking to have our hair styled in a particular way and must determine which hairdresser is best able to deliver the level of service we are seeking. On looking in the telephone directory we find that there are a considerable number of hairdressers from which to choose. When attempting to decide which particular hairdresser we will use, we are confronted with a number of difficulties. First, it is not like buying a more tangible product, such as a piece of hi-fi, a pair of shoes or an item of clothing. Each of these can be examined and tested before we make our final purchase. We can look at styling books and communicate to the hairdresser in considerable detail how we want our hair to look, but this is no guarantee that it will turn out exactly as we envisaged. Essentially we cannot pre-purchase a guaranteed level of service. This is in part owing to a second feature of services: their production commonly necessi-tates direct interaction between the supplier and customer. The purchaser is usually an essential part of the production process. For instance, in order for us to have our hair cut we have to physically visit the salon and sit in a chair while the hairdresser works. A haircut has to be experienced directly; we cannot send a substitute to have his or her hair cut on our behalf. The problem is that this interaction between the client and supplier creates a unique set of circumstances, which have a major impact on the creation and delivery of the service. Put simply, no two cus-tomers are alike. They may both want to look like Princess Diana but may have different shaped heads, different hair character-istics (wavy, straight, etc.) and different coloured hair. The hairdresser therefore has to attempt to create the same style in very different circumstances. Furthermore, their expectations may differ sharply. One customer may want a rough facsimile of the Princess Diana style, while the other may be attending a costume party and want as close a copy as possible. This illustrates a third feature of services: the difficulty of delivering a standardized service. The service supplier has to modify the output depending upon the different characteristics and needs of the purchasers. This implies that potential buyers of services are not able to make comparisons between the delivery of the same service, since they cannot expect to receive exactly the same service. We may enter a hairdressing salon and say, 'I have come to you because you gave my friend a great perm'. The problem is that there is no guarantee that the hairdresser will be able to recreate the same hair style or give an identical level of service. A different set of production circumstances has to be confronted since one element of the production process has changed: there is a different consumer. This leads to the fourth, and final, feature of service production: services are consumed at the point of delivery. Therefore, production and consumption occur simultaneously. We receive our haircut as the hairdresser opens and closes the scissors. These features imply that each transaction between a supplier and customer is unique, again making comparison and therefore quality control very difficult. As a result of these four service characteristics the purchase of a service always involves an element of uncertainty and risk.

Once the service has been delivered further difficulties arise, relating to the ability of a purchaser to evaluate the quality of the service. The main problem derives from one of the characteristics of services referred to above – their intangibility. At one extreme services do not take on a physical form. There may be nothing that can be seen, touched, tasted, heard or smelled. If services are not receptive to one of the five senses how is it possible for them to be evaluated? However, few, if any, services are wholly intangible. Most services contain, to some degree, an element of tangibility. For instance, in the case of a haircut the service is directed towards something tangible – our hair. In practice, when they are evaluating a service there is a tendency for customers to focus on the tangible outcomes, such as the look of their hair or the consultancy report. Where intangibles are evaluated they are usually of secondary importance. As a consequence, the evaluation of service quality is often at best a partial exercise that stresses the tangible elements. Thus, the greater the intangibility of the service the more difficult it is to verify its quality. If we are unable to evaluate the quality of a service once it has been

13

delivered then it is difficult to determine whether the actions taken by the service provider were necessary and appropriate. Did I really need to have my hair washed before it was cut? Did I need that special shampoo for dry hair? In such circumstances there is an opportunity for the service supplier, in this case a hairdresser, to oversell a service without us realizing that we are paying for unnecessary additional work. Furthermore, even if we were to discover that some aspect of the work undertaken on our behalf was unnecessary, it is impossible to return the service. This arises since, as mentioned above, a service is consumed at the point of delivery. Consequently, we cannot look into the mirror and say, 'This isn't what I asked for. Please take it back.' We have to wait for our natural hair colour to return or for our hair to grow. Our ability as consumers to evaluate the quality of a service is also made more difficult by the influence of external factors. For instance, as we leave the salon it might rain, with the consequence that the good work of the hairdresser is destroyed. The hairdresser may be sniffing because of a cold, which we find very irritating. This may influence our overall impression of the service delivered. Similarly, our experience of a sailing lesson is partly determined by the presence of wind. A lawyer may present every facet of our case accurately and to the best of his or her ability and still lose because of the vagaries of a judge and jury. An organizational change programme may fail, or falter, because of certain contingencies (e.g. a change of top management) that have a detrimental impact on the consultant's actions. These examples imply that the successful delivery of a service often requires additional elements, which are out of the supplier's control. Furthermore, the intangible nature of services may make it difficult for customers to disentangle those features for which the supplier has responsibility from those for which they do not. Thus, even if poor service quality is not the result of insufficient effort on the part of the service provider, it can be very difficult to convince angry clients that they are partly at fault.

The difficulties of selecting and evaluating the service of a management consultancy are further worsened by a number of structural characteristics of the management consultancy industry. The main problem is that it is relatively easy to establish a management consultancy. There are no effective barriers deterring entry into the industry. This has a number of consequences for clients of consultancy services. First, the number of alternative consultancies from which they can choose is growing, making the task of differentiating between potential suppliers even more difficult. Second, the ease of entry permits a wide range of organizations to offer consultancy services, ranging from accountancy firms to advertising and public relations consultancies. Hence, the choice available to clients is both large and wide. Clients therefore have to consider the advantages and disadvantages associated with using different types of consultancy organizations. Third, there is no quality threshold that consultancies have to overcome in order to enter the industry. As a consequence, the task of differentiating between high-and low-quality consultancies falls to the clients. This places considerable pressure on clients' abilities to select high-quality consultancies in the face of the difficulties enumerated above. Fourth, consultancies generally have short lives. In particular, the smaller the consultancy, the shorter is its life. Since the management consultancy industry is dominated by small firms this means that a large proportion of the consultancies operating in the industry are relatively new. This has two related implications for clients: (a) the composition of the pool of consultancies from which they make their final selection is constantly changing; and (b) in these circumstances it may not be possible to develop long-term relationships with consultancies. As a consequence, clients may often have to choose between consultancies of which they have little prior knowledge.

The aim of this book is to examine the causes of the problems endemic to the client – consultant relationship resulting from market and service characteristics, and then to suggest how these are alleviated or overcome in practice. Therefore, the book is concerned with discovering the answers to two key questions: (a) how do clients choose consultancies given the problems outlined above; (b) how do consultancies manage the relationship in such a way that they convince clients of the value and quality of their service? The framework of the argument presented in this book is illustrated in Figure 1.1

In exploring the first question a number of mechanisms are examined in terms of their ability to assist clients in determining

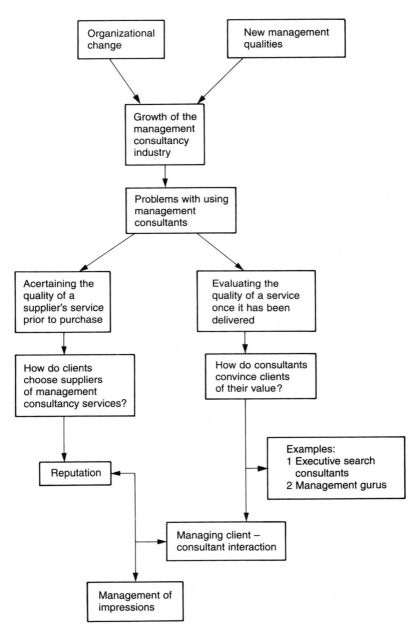

Figure 1.1 Framework of the argument

16

the quality of the different consultancies they may be considering. Three mechanisms are considered: contingency fees, regulation and reputation. The subsequent analysis suggests that clients primarily choose a management consultancy on the basis of its reputation, in addition to that of individual consultants. Reputation is a type of signalling activity in which the quality of services delivered in the past is used as an indicator of future quality. A good reputation is conferred on a consultancy or its consultants when clients perceive that they have consistently met their past promises. Suppliers who consistently deliver high-quality services tend to have good reputations. Such suppliers can be depended on to produce, time after time, the level and type of service that the client is seeking on each separate occasion. Client perceptions of service quality derive from two main sources: (a) previous experience of a particular supplier; and, (b) third-party recommendation. Clients, whether experienced or inexperienced users of consultancy services, prefer to transact with consultants and consultancies that they, or trusted informants, have used in the past.

In respect of the second question, if clients are buying management consultancy services from suppliers they, or valued informants, have used in the past, they must be convinced that they are receiving a high-quality service. What is the basis of this evaluation? What is it that leads clients to return to the same supplier or recommend the supplier to others? How do consultants successfully manage the client – consultant relationship, simultaneously enhancing their reputation and the likelihood of future transactions with the same client or referrals from existing clients? In essence, how do consultants give the impression that they have delivered a high quality service? In attempting to answer these questions the book argues that the key to an understanding of consultancy work and its success is to appreciate that successful consultancy, in its methods at least, recognizes, and indeed stresses, the active management of the client – consultant relationship. That is, successful consultancy is essentially about relationship management. As Levitt (1983: 111) writes, 'the sale merely consummates the courtship. Then the marriage begins. How good the marriage is depends on how well the relationship is managed by the seller.'

The book argues that at the core of successful consultancy is the art of impression management. If service characteristics, particularly intangibility, imply that a client will have difficulty in evaluating the quality of a service delivered, then there is scope for the consultant to construct a reality which persuades clients that they have purchased a valuable and high-quality service. Thus, each assignment provides an opportunity for a consultant to create or sustain his or her reputation. In order to identify the elements of the client – consultant relationship that underpin clients' evaluations of suppliers' quality the book examines the work of consultants in terms of the theatrical analogy (i.e. all the world is a stage) or dramaturgical metaphor. The aim here is to unfamiliarize the familiar and thus make it more knowable. Before we can understand how consultants seek to manage client perceptions of their quality and therefore the formation of their reputation, we need to 'see with different eyes'. The hope is that through the use of this metaphor readers will gain new insight and understanding into the work of consultants. They will 'actually come to *know* something instead of "knowing *about it*" ' (Burns, 1992: 109).

This conception of consultancy work is illustrated with reference to two types of consultancy activity: executive search (colloquially known as headhunting) and management gurus. These have been chosen because they highlight different features of the dramaturgical metaphor. Executive search consultants achieve success, and convince clients of their value and quality, by managing the 'back-stage' processes that lead up to the main event – the meeting between the client and candidates. Viewed in terms of the dramaturgical metaphor, executive search consultants can usefully be seen as impresarios, arranging and directing a certain sort of audition performance, managing impressions and limiting the dangers associated with 'risking character' – the candidates' and their own.

In contrast, the work of management gurus is a 'front stage' activity. They achieve success by giving a public performance that, via the use of a number of persuasive techniques, seeks to achieve transformations of consciousness in their audience of managers. Their performance is an exercise in persuasive communication; their aim the conversion of the audience to their way of thinking. Thus, managers become convinced of a management guru's value and quality through, and by, the process of conversion.

The argument developed in this book is grounded in six years of research into different aspects of the management consultancy market. The empirical results presented in this book therefore draw on several research projects which have sought to examine different aspects of the industry. The first part of this work was conducted between 1986 and 1990 and involved a detailed analysis of the supply of and demand for executive recruitment services in the UK. This work was founded on two major surveys. The first was directed at *all* UK executive recruitment consultancies[1]. The second questionnaire was mailed to the corporate personnel directors in *The Times Top 100 UK Companies*. Response rates of 42 and 55 per cent respectively were achieved. In addition, 72 structured face-to-face interviews were conducted with executive recruitment consultants and personnel directors to supplement the information obtained from the questionnaire surveys.

Subsequently, the focus of the research turned towards examining the activities of consultants who work closely with senior management to assist with the achievement of organizational change and renewal. This work was based on detailed interviews with 60 consultants and 25 clients. Both sets of interviews sought to examine the detail and dynamics of the client – consultant relationship. The aim was to try to determine the features that both parties believed were essential to a successful client – consultant relationship. The interviews with the 60 management consultancies were organized around the following issues:

- the methods of obtaining assignments;
- the conduct of the assignment;
- the identification of problems and their solution;
- a profile of consultancy in terms of its history, staff experience and range of services offered.

The interviews with the 25 clients sought to examine the same issues but from the other party's viewpoint. They therefore focused on:

- the process by which consultancies were chosen for particular assignments;
- the conduct of the assignment;
- the identification of problems and their solution;
- a historical profile of the organization's use of consultants.

In order to develop the argument elaborated earlier in this chapter the book is structured as follows. Chapter 2 identifies the major structural features of the management consultancy industry in order to provide an overall context for the later discussion and to determine their impact on the client – consultant relationship. Chapter 3 is concerned with identifying the key characteristics of services and examining how these impact on the client – consultant relationship. Chapter 4 seeks to answer the first question posed above: how do clients choose a supplier of management consultancy services? Three mechanisms – contingency fees, regulation and reputation – are critically examined in terms of their ability to assist clients to ascertain the relative quality of different suppliers of management consultancy services. Chapter 5 argues that the most appropriate way of understanding and analysing consultancy work is in terms of the theatrical analogy or dramaturgical metaphor. It argues that by using this metaphor the key features of what happens when clients and consultants meet and 'work' together are highlighted. Chapter 6 seeks to illuminate the work and role of consultants, in particular the activities of executive search consultants and management gurus, in terms of the dramaturgical metaphor. Aspects of their activities that convince clients of their value and quality are highlighted.

THE MANAGEMENT CONSULTANCY MARKET

Introduction

This chapter examines a number of structural features of the management consultancy industry. This analysis has two distinct, but nevertheless related, purposes. First, in identifying the key competitive features of the management consultancy industry it provides a backdrop from which the argument in subsequent chapters emanates. Three key structural features are identified: barriers to entry, heterogeneity and turbulence. Each of these is considered in turn. Second, using a framework for examining the competitive character of service industries initially suggested by Clark (1993a), the chapter seeks to explore how these market features impact on the client–consultant relationship. In particular, the discussion focuses on the difficulties associated with choosing a consultancy and evaluating the quality of the service once it has been delivered. These problems are seen to emanate primarily from the low level of barriers to entry into the management consultancy industry and the high levels of heterogeneity and industry turbulence.

In order to achieve these two aims the chapter is structured as follows. It begins by attempting to estimate the size of the UK management consultancy market. Three structural features are then examined in turn: barriers to entry, heterogeneity and turbulence. Finally, the general implications of these features for clients and consultancies are considered.

The management consultancy market

Market size

Estimating the size of the management consultancy market is an exercise fraught with difficulty owing to severe restrictions on the availability of appropriate data. Company accounts are of limited use since the great majority of management consultancies are private partnerships or sole traders with no legal obligation to publish their financial data. The study of 60 consultancies indicated that 10 per cent were public limited companies, 58 per cent were partnerships, 15 per cent were private limited companies, 13 per cent were sole traders and 3 per cent were trusts.

Industry bodies are a further source of data on consultancy revenues, since in the UK the Management Consultancies Association (MCA), in the *President's Statement and Annual Report*, publishes the aggregate fees of its member organizations. Over the past 30 years these have grown dramatically. In 1960 the combined revenues of MCA members were £6 million; in 1980 these had grown to £61.8 million; by 1993 they were a massive £868.3 million. In real terms MCA members' fees increased by a little under 1,200 per cent between 1960 and 1993. However, the extent to which these figures reflect the 'real' or actual size of the UK management consultancy market is limited by two factors. First, the membership of the MCA is skewed towards the larger and more long-established consultancies. Indeed, the MCA was formed in 1956 by Inbucon, PA, P-E and Urwick Orr as an association for 'the leading management consulting firms in the United Kingdom' (Management Consultancies Association, 1994:1). Second, membership is currently limited to 35 organizations. While these organizations account for a substantial proportion of consultancy revenues in the UK, anywhere between 45 and 65 per cent (Schlegelmilch *et al.*, 1992: 47), the industry also comprises many thousands of smaller consultancies.

A third major source of data is the number of management consultancies registering for VAT. Management consultancies are classified into VAT trade classification (VTC) 8655. However, these data have two serious limitations. First, the management consultancy industry is mainly comprised of small firms, some of whom – an indeterminate number – are exempt from VAT because they trade below the mandatory threshold for registration, currently £46,000. Second, firms are categorized into each VAT trade classification according to their principal and defining activity. Yet, as will be shown later in this chapter, for many organizations engaging in management consultancy it is a secondary activity. Since no account is taken of the range and type of services offered by organizations, the VAT statistics exclude those management consultancy services which are secondary to the principal, and defining, activity. As a consequence, they underestimate the size of the industry. Despite these limitations, the data on VAT registrations remain the most all-encompassing, although still incomplete, statistical profile of the industry. Using these data Keeble *et al.* (1994: 6) have suggested that in 1990 the UK management consultancy industry comprised 11,777 firms with a combined turnover of a little over £2.5 billion. Although a little out of date, given the data problems outlined above, this is currently the most reliable estimate of the size of the management consultancy industry in the UK.

Barriers to entry

Barriers to entry are an important determinant of the structure of any industry. By governing the manner and rate of entry they determine both the shape and the competitive character of an industry. While the management consultancy industry has its origins in the early part of this century in the time-and-motion studies of Frank B. Gilbreth (1869–1924) and the scientific management principles of Frederick W. Taylor (1856–1915), as the previous chapter indicated its expansion has mainly occurred in the past 40 years, with the pace quickening considerably in the 1980s. For instance, in 1956 four companies – Inbucon (established in 1926), Urwick, Orr and Partners (established in 1934), P-E Consulting Group (established in 1934) and PA Management

Consultants (established in 1943) – accounted for three-quarters of the £4 million consultancy market in the UK (Tisdall, 1982: 9). However, by 1990, as mentioned above, there were a little under 12,000 consultancies operating in the industry. Bryson *et al.* (1993: 121) report that 57 per cent of these management consultancies had been established since 1980. Furthermore, as Table 2.1 shows, 62 per cent of the 60 consultancies that participated in the research study had entered since 1980. The explosion in the number of management consultancies in recent years indicates that both the method and the speed of entry have been significant determinants of the industry's structure.

Any discussion of barriers to entry is not possible without a definition of the term. A narrow definition, such as that used by Bain (1956) in his seminal study *Barriers to New Competition*, focuses solely on the establishment of completely new firms (i.e. they did not exist in any other legal form prior to entry) in an industry. This definition of entry has a number of deficiencies following from the view that entry is effected only by 'newborn' firms. First, it excludes 'cross-entry' as a legitimate form of entry. This refers to the movement of firms between distinctive markets. Examples of this form of entry include newspaper publishers establishing a presence in the television industry, retailers entering the financial services market, cable operators entering the telecommunications market and so forth. It will be demonstrated later in the chapter that cross-entry is a major source of entry in the management consultancy industry. Second, it excludes entry via take-over or merger since neither of these would expand the capacity of the industry. To take account of these deficiencies Hines (1957) defined entry as the production of a good or service that is perfectly substitutable in the minds of purchasers. However, some firms are considered such a threat that the mere expression of an intention to expand into a new market can produce defensive reactions from existing participants. Consider the restructuring of cross-Channel ferry operators that followed the announcement of the plan to build the Channel Tunnel. Hence, entry can be viewed as a process that upsets the equilibrium of existing market conditions. This does not have to be the result of direct competition. Thus, barriers to entry are obstacles that prevent potential entrants from disturbing the character of existing market competition, i.e. they isolate the market from potentially disruptive forces. In the case of the management consultancy industry, barriers to entry prevent potential entrants from obtaining assignments. Once an assignment has been awarded to an organization, regardless of its patrimony, the organization is deemed to have entered the industry.

The height of barriers to entry is defined as the relative disadvantages of potential entrants compared to established firms in the market. Five types of barrier to entry may be discerned in the management consultancy industry: absolute cost advantages, initial capital requirements, scale barriers, product differentiation and legal barriers. These may be grouped more generally under two headings: cost and structural barriers. Cost barriers can be further subdivided into 'natural' and 'artificial' barriers. The discussion now turns to consider the nature and relevance of each barrier to the management consultancy industry.

Natural cost barriers
Natural cost barriers exist even in the absence of potential entry. Hence, they do not arise from retaliatory action by established consultancies responding to the potential threat of entry. Rather, they are an implicit feature of the industry. Three types of natural cost barriers may be discerned: absolute cost barriers, initial capital requirements and scale barriers. The implications of each for the management consultancy industry are discussed below.

Absolute cost barriers occur when established management consultancies can operate at a lower cost than prospective entrants. This applies regardless of the size of the consultancy. The economics literature suggests that the potential bases for such advantages may arise from one, or a combination, of the following sources.

1 Established consultancies may control superior production techniques, which are protected through patents, secrecy and the knowledge that comes from experience.
2 Existing firms may own or control key resources necessary for the delivery of the service. As a consequence, potential

entrants may be barred from access to these resources, may have to pay a higher price for them or may have to use inferior supplies.
3 Potential entrants may have to pay more for initial capital relative to established consultancies.

Such barriers are unlikely to arise in the management consultancy industry, since the industry is not characterized by asset specificity. This relates to the ease with which assets can be put to alternative uses. For instance, in the railway industry the track is characterized by high asset specificity since it can only carry trains and rolling stock. In contrast, the asset specificity, of the rolling stock is lower, since it may be put to a number of alternative uses. It can be used to carry passengers, coal, iron ore and so on. The key assets within the management consultancy industry include the intellectual assets of consultants, support staff (e.g. researchers) and administrative staff. These can be applied to a wide range of industries. Similarly, physical assets, which include office space, computers, telephones, etc., are not industry specific. Therefore, new entrants are unlikely to pay more for such assets since incumbents have no monopoly over the supply of these resources.

Initial capital requirements refer to the initial costs of establishing a management consultancy. Bain (1956) argues that new entrants will have difficulty in obtaining initial amounts of capital since banks are reluctant to finance new business ventures, particularly in highly competitive markets such as the management consultancy industry. If a firm manages to secure finance it may have to pay a higher rate of interest, which reflects the additional risk, and so have an absolute cost barrier. This is more likely if the amount of the initial capital is large. Hence, this barrier is dependent upon the size of the investment required to establish a new enterprise.

The management consultancy industry is not capital intensive. The basic requirements for operating include a telephone, fax, stationery, secretarial support and an office. Many consultancies operate from individuals' homes and share secretarial services. Indeed, the latter can be purchased on a 'when needs must' basis. However, for new entrants that have entered via acquisition or merger, such as a number of the large accountancy firms, the cost of entry has been considerably higher. For example, Peat Marwick Mitchell acquired Drake Shehan in 1983, Ayres Whitemore in the same year, KMG Main Hudson in 1986 and Nolan Norton in 1987. Price Waterhouse acquired Urwick Orr and Management Horizons in 1984. Other accountancy firms such as Arthur Young, Coopers & Lybrand and Touche Ross, acquired at least two consultancies each during the 1980s (Syrett, 1988).

Scale barriers occur when a new entrant has to establish a large amount of capacity, relative to total industry output, in order to produce at a competitive cost. The amount of capacity needed to achieve economies of scale may be a large proportion of industry demand. Hence, an additional output of this size may drive down the market price to a level where costs cannot be covered if existing firms maintain their pre-entry levels of output. In order for scale barriers to be high, firms must have to enter at a large size, producing a large proportion of industry output. However, the majority of management consultancies in the UK are small firms. In the study of the UK management consultancy industry by Bryson *et al.* (1993), 77 per cent of consultancies employed 12 or fewer consultants. Clark (1993b), in a study of one sector of the management consultancy industry, reports that the average size of an executive search consultancy is four consultants. The 60 management consultancies that participated in the second phase of the author's research had an average of six consultants.

Artificial cost barriers
Artificial cost barriers are responsive barriers. They arise through actions taken by existing firms in response to the threat of entry. Product differentiation is an example of this type of barrier. This is commonly defined as the degree to which customers (in this case clients) distinguish between different services and service providers. As a consequence, there is imperfect substitution between different services, since they are not perfectly substitutable in the minds of buyers. Differing levels of quality, consumer ignorance, product prestige and advertising are all important sources of product differentiation. However, within the framework of barriers to entry theory, product differentiation

has a more specific meaning. In this instance it refers to the preference of buyers for the services of existing suppliers (i.e. management consultancies) over those of potential or new entrants.

Product differentiation barriers arise from a number of sources, including the accumulated preferences of buyers, control of unique product features through patent protection, ownership and control of the distribution system and the cost and time of developing a high quality reputation. In his seminal study of entry barriers in 14 industries, Bain (1956) concluded that product differentiation was the largest source of barriers to entry in five industries and parts of two further industries. Similarly, Mann's (1966) study of entry barriers in 30 industries suggested that product differentiation was an important source of barriers to entry. However, Clarke (1985) has argued that the importance of product differentiation barriers is limited to the initial 'break-in' period. He argues that once a service is established in the minds of buyers, product differentiation is no longer a significant disadvantage. Hence, the 'break-in' cost is the source of the barrier.

A number of studies have reported that the reputation of a consultancy and its consultants is the most important criterion identified by clients to select between consultancies (Stock and Zinszer, 1987; Askvik, 1992; Dawes *et al.*, 1992; Clark, 1993b).[1] It would therefore be expected that this barrier might be high. If it were not, new consultancies would enter the high quality, high price, end of the market by charging lower fees and forcing existing fee levels down. However, O'Farrell *et al.* (1993: 44) suggest three reasons to explain why this is a difficult entry strategy to pursue. First, creating a reputation can be costly and time consuming. A track-record is a prerequisite for the development of a high quality reputation.[2] Second, new entrants have to convince clients that their quality matches that of incumbent consultancies. This is difficult since, as will be suggested in the next chapter, a major transaction cost is buyer uncertainty resulting from the imbalance of information between buyers and sellers. The seller is better informed about the quality of the service than the buyer. Buyer ignorance means that buyers are unable to distinguish between the relative qualities of different consultancies. Hence, even if a new entrant were able to deliver a high quality service, from the clients' viewpoint their service would be indistinguishable from that of a low quality producer. Third, and related to the previous point, the nature of services, particularly intangibility and perishability, reinforces the importance of reputation as a primary selection criterion. Hence, incumbent consultancies maintain their stock of 'goodwill' with clients by investing heavily in signalling their quality to existing and potential buyers. This creates not only additional costs for new entrants but also certain rigidities, in that buyers may prefer transacting with known consultancies to risking the new and unfamiliar (Nayyar, 1990). Established consultancies are therefore able to charge higher fees and reap higher returns than new entrants who may be of equal quality.

Structural barriers
Structural barriers set the framework within which entry occurs. They are a series of filters which determine those firms that have the necessary requisites for entry. Once the various structural barriers are surmounted, potential entrants then encounter the barriers enumerated above. For instance, legal barriers set the parameters for entry. They provide an over-arching framework within which potential entrants are compelled to proceed. In the management consultancy industry no specific legal entry restrictions exist. No pre-entry qualifications are necessary. For example, there is no industry body determining the content and certification of management consultancy skills and knowledge.[3] A consultancy need only obtain an assignment to have entered the industry and therefore become a management consultancy. The following statements, taken from interviews with three management consultants, indicate the ease of entry into the industry.

> I worked for another consultancy for five years. Two years ago I left and set up my own firm. . .I had an established reputation and found that several of my clients followed me.

> I was made redundant but within a few weeks a former colleague called and asked if I could provide a specific input

Managing consultants

Table 2.1 Entry into the UK management consultancy industry, 1965–1990

Year	New entrants	Cross-entry		
		Subsidiaries of foreign consultancies	Divisions of accountancy firms	Divisions of other UK firms
1965	1			
1966				
1967	1			
1968		1		
1969				
1970				
1971	1	1	1	
1972	1			
1973	2		1	
1974		1		
1975				
1976	1	1		
1977		1	1	
1978	2		2	
1979				
1980	1	1		
1981	2	1		1
1982	1		2	
1983	1	2	1	1
1984	2	1	2	
1985	1			
1986	1	1	2	1
1987	3		2	
1988	4		1	1
1989	2		1	
1990	2			
Total	29	11	16	4
Per cent	48	18	27	7

on a consultancy job he had. From that start I subsequently developed my own consultancy business.

I used to be a senior personnel manager in several retail organizations. On retiring from my last job I established my own consultancy offering a range of personnel consultancy services.

Having discussed the height of individual barriers, we now turn to an analysis of the nature and incidence of entry into the UK management consultancy industry.

The nature and incidence of entry
The above discussion identified the importance of a number of barriers to entry in the management consultancy industry and assessed the extent to which potential entrants were disadvantaged by each barrier. However, because individual barriers may act simultaneously, the deterrent effect of each barrier cannot be calculated. Rather the nature and incidence of entry reflects the combined effects of all barriers discussed above. Evidence of the pattern of entry into the management consultancy industry between 1965 and 1993 is presented in Table 2.1.[4]

In Table 2.1, 48 per cent of consultancies were entirely 'new' entrants. These are defined as 'new' independent firms that are not subsidiaries of existing firms. Hines (1957) referred to these as 'newborn' firms. Table 2.1 further indicates that 52 per cent of these management consultancies were cross-entrants. It was established in the previous discussion that cross-entry refers to the establishment of a legal entity new to the industry by a firm already established in another market, i.e. an established outside firm. Three types of cross-entry in the management consultancy industry can be distinguished.

1 A UK subsidiary of a foreign-owned consultancy – 18 per cent of the management consultancies were branch offices of foreign consultancies. This figure indicates the importance of foreign, in particular American, consultancies to the development of the UK management consultancy industry. For example, American consultancy firms such as Arthur D. Little, Bain & Co., Booz, Allen & Hamilton, Boston Consulting Group

and McKinsey are all major players in the UK management consultancy industry.

2 An additional service offered by UK-based accountancy firms – 27 per cent of the management consultancies entered the industry via this route. This indicates both the low level of entry barriers identified in the previous discussion and the importance of this sector to the recent expansion of the industry.

3 An additional service offered by other UK organizations – 7 per cent of management consultancies entered via this route. This suggests that to date entry via this route has been a rare occurrence.

Economic theory suggests that the impact of the height of barriers to entry differs depending on the type of entrant. Different types of entrant suffer different degrees of disadvantage, 'Newborn' firms would be the most disadvantaged, with cross-entrants the least hindered. Therefore, it would follow that the bulk of entry would be from cross-entrants rather than new firms. Yet this is contradicted by the evidence presented in Table 2.1. A large percentage of the entry from the group of consultancies participating in the study was from 'new' firms, supposedly the most disadvantaged. This may have occurred for two reasons.

First, the lack of any substantial entry barriers supports new entry. Entry is in effect 'free' (Bevan, 1974). The earlier discussion has established that barriers to entry are so low they fail to deter entry effectively. Second, many new entrants are perhaps not strictly 'newborn' firms. In the group of consultancies participating in the study all the new management consultancies were staffed by consultants previously experienced in industry. Given these findings it is likely that many of the new, independently established consultancies are the result of consultants leaving established operations and establishing their own consultancies, i.e. fragmentation. These consultancies, while being new legal entities, have certain cross-entrant advantages, such as existing knowledge, established reputation and client contacts. Indeed, fragmentation is a form of cross-entry by individuals rather than by firms.

Heterogeneity

The low barriers to entry detailed above have enabled a wide variety of firms to enter the management consultancy industry. The discussion of the incidence of entry indicated that 52 per cent of management consultancies were cross-entrants. This implies that a major structural characteristic of the industry is the heterogeneity of firms offering management consultancy services. Indeed, the industry is characterized by low levels of exclusiveness (the extent to which firms offer a single service and so are present in a single market) and high levels of specialization (the extent to which firms offer a range of services and so are present in more than one market) (Evely and Little, 1960: 31–2). Two main types of management consultancies operate in the UK.

The first are specialist management consultancies, which are distinguished from the other types in that their primary source of income is from management consultancy assignments. Peet (1988: 7) has suggested that the services offered by these consultancies can be divided into four general areas: (a) strategy; (b) traditional; (c) human resources; and (d) specialist (e.g. executive recruitment). Much of the previous literature has focused exclusively on these types of consultancies. However, failure to recognize the diversity of organizations offering management consultancy services to date has resulted in an incomplete understanding of the industry dynamics.

The second are multi-service organizations that offer a range of services, of which management consultancy is one. Management consultancy activities are therefore secondary to their principal, and defining, activity. In the main these organizations include: (a) the consultancy divisions of the large accountancy firms; and (b) the consultancy divisions of large communications groups.

The diversification of large accountancy firms into management consultancy, and related services, has been well documented (see Daniels *et al.* 1988). While audit fees have generally remained their single most important source of income, they are a declining proportion. For example, in the UK in 1992–3 Arthur Andersen derived a little over 56 per cent of its total fee income from consultancy fees. Coopers and Lybrand, KPMG Peat Marwick and Price Waterhouse earned in excess of 20 per cent of their total fees from consultancy activities (*Accountancy*, 1993: 13). The position of accountancy firms is now so dominant that, according to the magazine *Management Consultancy* (Abbott, 1995: 16), they account for six of the ten largest management consultancies in the UK, with Andersen Consulting, Coopers and Lybrand, and Ernst & Young occupying the first three places.

During the 1980s a number of large communication groups diversified into the management consultancy industry via acquisition. Some of the most well known examples include Saatchi and Saatchi's purchase of Hay-MSL, Moxon Dolphin & Kerby, and Harrison Cowley; the purchase of Accountancy Personnel, a specialist recruitment consultancy, by the Hays Group (primarily a transport and distribution company); and the establishment of 3i Consultants by 3i, the UK's leading source of venture capital (Underwood, 1989).

Turbulence

A further indicator of the extent to which entry is free in an industry is the measure of industry turbulence. Turbulence indicates the 'the flux created in an industry's total composition by flows of births and deaths' (Beesley and Hamilton, 1984: 220). An industry's turbulence, expressed as a T value, is calculated as the sum of births and deaths in an industry divided by the stock of firms in the base year. A T value indicates the percentage of firms that have entered or exited an industry between two points in time. Hence, turbulence measures the degree to which an industry's total composition changes over time. It is therefore a good indicator of the extent to which the length of firms' lifespans vary between different industries. Highly turbulent industries are characterized by a greater incidence of births and deaths; firms in these industries have short lifespans. Conversely, in industries where turbulence is low the turnover of firms (i.e. their birth and death rate) is less frequent and their lifespans are correspondingly longer.

Table 2.2 indicates that in the early part of the 1980s the business service sector in the UK was highly turbulent with a mean T value of 41 per cent and a range of 20 to 82 per cent. This

Table 2.2 Turbulence in the business service sector, 1980–1983

Ranking	VTC	Industry	Turbulence (%)
1	8653	Computer services	82
2	7080	Post, telecommunications	60
3	8655	Management consultants	47
4	8657	Duplicating, calculating, typewriting agencies	40
5	8640	Advertising, market research	39
6	8656	Staff bureaux, employment agencies	38
7	8653, 8659	Other services, including firms acting as chartered and company secretaries	37
8	8654	Contract cleaning	28
9	8651	Industrial and commercial valuers	20

Note: Turbulence is the annual percentage of births + deaths divided by the stock of firms in the base year.
Source: Batstone (1991).

compares with a global T value of 37 per cent reported by Beesley and Hamilton (1984) for a sample of manufacturing industries.

The T value for management consultants is above the average for the business service sector as a whole and indicates that, between 1980 and 1983, 47 per cent of consultancies were either entering or exiting the industry. These figures confirm the existence of low entry and exit barriers within the management consultancy industry.

Keeble *et al.'s* (1994) study of the management consultancy industry suggests that turbulence is particularly prevalent among smaller consultancies. They report a T value for the industry between 1985 and 1990 of 36 per cent. However, the five year (1985–90) T value for firms employing no more than two consultants was 51 per cent, with a T value of 42 per cent for consultancies employing between three and five consultants, a T value of 27 per cent for consultancies employing between six and

Table 2.3 Implications of the key market features for management consultants and their clients

Key market features	Implications for management consultants	Implications for clients
Barriers to entry	Entry simple to effect. Large and expanding number of industry participants. Intense competition.	Large number of service suppliers. No formal assessment of suppliers' quality prior to entering the industry. Client responsible for the determination of supplier quality.
Heterogeneity	Possible to offer a wide range of services. Competing with a diverse range of organizations.	Wide variety of alternative service suppliers and service offerings. Information banks on suppliers can become quickly outdated.
Turbulence	Life expectancy short for smaller consultancies.	Difficult to develop long-term relationships with smaller consultancies unless identify survivors.

12 consultants, and a T value of 23 per cent for consultancies employing between thirteen and twenty-five consultants. In contrast, no consultancy employing more than 100 consultants closed over the period.

Implications for clients and consultants

Table 2.3 shows the implications that these market features have for consultancies and their clients. The previous discussion suggested that the key structural feature within the management consultancy industry is the low level of barriers to entry. This in turn underpins the high levels of heterogeneity and turbulence within the industry. The ineffectiveness of entry barriers has three implications for management consultancies.

First, entry can be effected with ease, suggesting that there is little, if anything, to stop someone establishing a management consultancy. We could all have business cards and stationery printed which described us as a management consultant and then erect a shingle announcing this. However, this does not in itself guarantee that we will be successful in obtaining assignments. Second, low barriers to entry enabled the industry to expand rapidly as more and more potential entrants sought to join what was perceived as a potentially lucrative occupation, where demand outstripped supply. Third, the recent expansion in the numbers of organizations offering management consultancy services has resulted in an intensely competitive market place as over-demand has gradually been replaced by over-supply. This has coincided with a deep recession in the first few years of the 1990s, which, according to an article in *The Economist* (Peet 1988), has threatened the continuing growth of consultancy revenues, resulted in an increasing number of consultants being made redundant and led to 'the talk among consultancy firms [being] of take-overs and mergers' (p. 81).

For clients the ease of entry means that there is a myriad of consultancies from which they can make their final selection. There is a large number of potential alternatives that can be considered before the client alights on one supplier. In addition, there is no formal initial assessment of a consultancy's competence or quality prior to entry. Consultancies do not have to overcome a pre-entry quality threshold in order to operate in the industry. There is no minimum standard of quality that all consultancies are obliged to offer. Rather, the quality of a consultancy's service is something that clients have to determine when choosing between alternative suppliers of consultancy services. The lack of any structural barriers therefore places considerable emphasis on a client's ability to distinguish between high and low quality consultancies prior to contracting with a particular consultancy.

Since entry is virtually free (i.e. costless), a heterogeneous collection of firms offer management consultancy services. These range from firms that specialize in management consultancy activities to divisions of accountancy firms, advertising agencies and public relations consultancies. Hence, clients have both a large and a wide range of alternatives from which to select.

A major outcome of the competitive conditions within the industry is the high level of industry turbulence among smaller consultancies. Since the majority of management consultancies are small firms this has a significant impact on the composition of the industry. For a large proportion of the industry active participation tends to be short. This may indicate a fly-by-night strategy on the part of the smaller (and the majority of) consultancies within the industry. They may enter the industry to extract a quick profit and then withdraw. These consultancies tend to be motivated by the opportunity of earning a quick return. They are not concerned with their clients' long-term interests. Each additional assignment is viewed as a further profit-taking opportunity. As a consequence, the commitment of these consultancies to offering a high quality service is likely to be low. They will tend to focus on extracting a quick return prior to making a quick exit.

Industry turbulence also has implications for clients of consultancy services. The influx of new firms implies that each time a client dips into the market the pool of consultancies from which it is able to select has changed as new firms enter and others leave. As a consequence, clients' information banks on suppliers can become quickly outdated. To avoid this situation clients are having continually to replenish their information banks in order to incorporate data on consultancies that were previously unknown to them. If they fail to do this they will be making a selection decision when they know little about the alternatives they are considering. Furthermore, as they modify their data banks in order to take account of intra-industry movements, clients are left with an ever-diminishing number of consultancies that may be classified as 'stayers' or 'survivors'. Long-term relationships may only be possible with this group of consultancies. Relationships with consultancies outside of this group may therefore be short-lived.

Conclusion

This chapter has sought to identify the main structural features of the management consultancy industry and to enumerate their potential effects on the client–consultant relationship. Three structural features were examined in turn: barriers to entry, heterogeneity and turbulence. It was argued that the low level of barriers to entry has underpinned the rapid expansion of the industry in recent times. New consultancies can enter the industry with ease. Entry is in effect free. For clients of management consultancy services this means that any assessment of a consultancy's quality has to be made once entry has been effected, since there is no formal mechanism relating to the certification of consultancy skills and providing some indication of potential quality prior to entry. This arises because there are no structural barriers to entry in the management consultancy industry. Therefore, the quality of a consultancy's service has to be ascertained before purchase. Since there is no certificating body endorsing an industry-wide standard of quality, the responsibility for pre-judging the quality of a consultancy's service falls to the clients. Hence, their ability to ascertain the quality of a consultancy's service prior to purchase is of crucial importance.

The low level of entry barriers underpins the high level of heterogeneity within the industry. The ease of entry has enabled a large number of organizations from the accountancy, advertising and public relations industries to offer management consultancy services. This suggests that the pre-contractual stage is not simply characterized by a condition of large numbers bidding. In addition, clients have a *wide* range of alternatives from which to choose. They must therefore determine the pros and cons associated with using different kinds of suppliers of management consultancy services. This adds a further level of complexity to the initial selection decision.

Finally, the high level of industry turbulence among smaller consultancies implies that there is no certainty that clients will be able to transact with the same supplier at some point in the future, since the industry is characterized by considerable fluidity in its composition. The industry is constantly being regenerated by the influx of new consultancies and the death of existing participants. The result is that the management consultancy industry includes many small firms with short lives. When clients use these consultancies they may have difficulty developing a continuous, long-term, relationship with a single supplier. Where this is the case clients may have to switch between alternative suppliers. However, depending on the extent of the changes to the composition of the industry, their information banks on suppliers may have little relevance to the new selection context. Where their information banks fail to reflect the current state of the market, clients, even experienced ones, will in effect be first-time purchasers since they will be selecting between consultancies that are unknown to them. To avoid this clients need to refresh their information banks before each purchase decision. Since this can be a costly and lengthy procedure, purchasers of management consultancy services are likely to find a mechanism that enables them to circumvent this problem.

3

THE CHARACTERISTICS OF MANAGEMENT CONSULTANCY SERVICES

Introduction

This chapter builds on Chapter 2 in that it takes as its starting point the notion that clients are responsible for ascertaining the quality of the service offered by potential suppliers of management consultancy services. This arises since there is no formal assessment of a consultancy's competence or quality before entering the industry. As a consequence, high and low quality consultancies can operate simultaneously in the market for management consultancy services. The skill of the client is to be able to distinguish between them. This in turn is dependent upon the availability, accuracy and clarity of information about the consultancies they may be considering prior to purchase. However, a number of service characteristics imply that the quality of a consultancy's service is difficult to ascertain prior to purchase and to evaluate once delivered. Hence, whereas the seller may know the quality of the service, the buyer often does not. In particular, services are intangible and so quality is difficult to observe, measure and ascertain; service production is inherently social, resulting from the inseparability of production and consumption;

services are not standardized implying variability in service output; and services are perishable and so cannot be stored. The purpose of this chapter is to examine how these features impact on the delivery of management consultancy services. In exploring and developing these issues the chapter divides into two parts. The first part identifies four service characteristics: intangibility, interaction, heterogeneity and perishability. Each of these is discussed in turn before their implications for the market provision of such services as management consultancy are determined. The second part of the chapter focuses on the implications of each of these service characteristics for the delivery and evaluation of management consultancy services.

Service characteristics

Management theorists have argued that services share a number of common characteristics which differentiate them from goods. The characteristics most commonly distinguished by these commentators are intangibility, interaction, heterogeneity and perishability. Each of these features as it relates to services is considered in greater detail below.

Intangibility

This is perhaps the most commonly identified characteristic of services and as such is considered by some commentators to be the factor that best distinguishes them from material goods. At its simplest this means that while services are intangible, goods are tangible. Hence, prior to the purchase of a service a consumer is unable to perceive a complete physical form. There is nothing that can be seen, touched, tasted, heard or smelled. Oberoi and Hales (1990: 701–2) write: 'this means that there is no complete physical form which can be perceived by the consumer at the pre-purchase stage, as an object or thing'. Similarly, Walker (1985: 48) suggests that services and goods primarily differ in that services 'do not take the intervening form of a material product'.

However, a number of writers have questioned whether the

concept of intangibility, while it is an important service characteristic, is perhaps too rigid and therefore fails to take account of the
extent to which certain goods contain intangible elements and a
number of services produce tangible outputs. For example,
Wilson (1972) has suggested that the characteristic of tangibility
can be divided into 'pure intangible' services (e.g. education,
communication), services that add value to a tangible product
(e.g. decorators, launderettes) and services that supply a tangible
product (e.g. financial services and retailing). Similarly, Shostak
(1977: 73) writes: 'It is wrong to imply that services are just like
products 'except' for intangibility. By such logic, apples are just
like oranges, except for their 'appleness'. She sought to overcome
this problem by locating services on a continuum, with the
extremes of 'tangible dominant' (e.g. soft drinks) and 'intangible
dominant' (e.g. teaching). Consulting is positioned towards the
end of the intangible dominant side of the scale.

These writers raise the question as to whether it is constructive
to distinguish between goods and services in terms of their
intangibility. Building on this argument, Levitt (1981) suggests
that more progress may be possible if, instead of differentiating
between goods and services, one refers to intangibles and
tangibles. He argues that all products, whether manufactured
goods or services, possess some degree of intangibility. Hence, it
is more useful to distinguish a *continuum of intangibility*. This
ranges from one extreme of highly intangible products (e.g.
accounting, consulting, films and travel) to another of highly
tangible products (e.g. cars, aircraft engines, buildings). The
latter can usually be experienced to some degree – perhaps seen,
touched, smelled, tasted or even tested – prior to purchase. For
example, it is possible to test-drive a car, test aircraft engines
before installation and visit a building prior to occupation.
However, even the apparently most tangible products, such as
factory machinery, plant equipment, computers and washing
machines, possess intangible features which cannot be reliably
tested or experienced in advance of consumption. These include
delivery on time, correct installation, training in correct operation, servicing, repair and maintenance work, which are all
critical to the product's successful operation. Furthermore, these
intangible features (i.e. the service content) are an important

aspect of the consumer's favourable evaluation of the product and are therefore a key feature of its success.

Products which have a higher intangible component (primarily services) tend to be more labour-intensive in their production and delivery. Levitt (1981) suggests that this creates a number of special problems. First, there is more scope for errors, idiosyncrasies and delays leading to greater customer disappointment. Conversely, a more tangible product, manufactured under close supervision, is more likely than an intangible one to fulfil customer expectations. Second, organizations producing highly intangible products have greater quality control problems. The high level of personal discretion makes it more difficult to provide consistent quality. The quality of a service may therefore vary depending upon who is performing it. Third, customers of intangible products *'usually don't know what they're getting until they don't get it'* (Levitt, 1981: 100). This implies that customers only become aware of intangible products once there is a break-down of some kind in the delivery. This suggests that customers of intangibles are more aware of failure than success. Hence, the successful delivery of an intangible product to a customer may go unnoticed and uncredited.

Flipo (1988) suggests that one way of overcoming the fact that goods and services are, in varying degrees, intangible is to concentrate on 'what is universally immaterial in services. . .the *performance* of the service itself' (p. 287). This is echoed by Rathwell (1974: 58) who writes that 'goods are produced, services are performed' (cited in Levitt, 1981: 98). This element of service delivery refers to the overall experience of a consumer derived solely from the 'expressive equipment' of the service provider rather than any material good to which the service is attached. Such features may include a person's appearance, posture, speech, facial expressions, bodily gestures and the like. All of these are intimately connected to the actions of the service provider. For instance, a driving lesson may be enhanced by the fact that a learner driver is 'at the wheel' of a particular vehicle, but his or her confidence and driving acumen are also related to the general demeanour of the instructor. The way in which the instructor comports him or herself, whether as a nervous or a confident passenger, will inevitably impact on the actions of the learner. Subsequent chapters in this book argue similarly that the 'appearance' and 'manner' of a management consultant is a central feature of the client – consultant relationship, and as such is a primary determinant of the former's evaluation of the service delivered by the latter. Both these terms were first coined by Goffman (1990). 'Appearance' refers to the features of an individual that indicate his or her role during a particular interactive episode (e.g. learner or instructor, client or consultant). 'Manner' relates to the character a person takes when giving a particular performance. For instance, a person may be chatty, quiet, reserved, humorous and the like. Each of these will give an impression of what is expected of the other interactant and so taint his or her experience of the performance and underpin the evaluation of the service.

Implicit within this conception of performance is the notion of service as an experience founded upon the interaction, or interface, between the buyer and seller. Social intercourse is a necessary part of service production and consumption. To use the theatrical metaphor, a service performance is dependent upon the presence and interaction of the 'actors' and 'audience'. This idea will be developed more fully in later chapters, for the moment the discussion turns to the nature of interaction within services.

Interaction

As suggested above, a further distinguishing feature of service delivery is that it is primarily a process of interaction between the buyer and seller. In order for the delivery of a service to be complete the buyer and seller frequently have to interact directly. Hence, the production and consumption of a service is often based on the interaction between the buyer and seller. The delivery of a service may therefore be characterized as a relational activity based upon social intercourse between the two parties.

O'Farrell and Hitchens (1990: 167) suggest that there are three basic types of interaction between buyers and sellers.

1 The producer and consumer are separate throughout the delivery of the service, such as information services available over the telephone, via a computer or in the post.

2 Customers may serve themselves using equipment or procedures supplied by the producer, such as a photocopier, clothes pattern or self-assembly furniture.
3 The producer and consumer produce the service in interaction with one another, so that each has an impact on the outcome; for example, a haircut, a driving or sailing lesson, a medical consultation.

While the importance of the first two forms of interaction is recognized, the focus of this book is on consultancy activities, which require direct contact between the client and consultant. Without this the service cannot be produced, since there would be no performance as the performer and audience would remain disaggregated entities (Schechner, 1977: 142). The following discussion will therefore concentrate on the last type of interaction.

Mills and Margulies (1980) have sought to classify service organizations in terms of the nature of interaction between buyers and sellers. They distinguish between three types of service organizations: maintenance-interactive, task-interactive and personal interactive. 'Maintenance-interactive' organizations are characterized by a 'cosmetic, continuous interaction between employee and customer/client in which the focal point is building trust or confidence in an attempt by the organization to sustain the relationship for an indefinite time period' (Mills and Margulies, 1980: 260). In pursuing this objective the organization projects an image of stability with routinized service delivery (e.g. banks and building societies). Hence, the relationship between such organizations and their clients tends to be limited to a small number of standardized events (e.g. depositing and withdrawing money) which only permit surface-level interaction.

In contrast, in 'task-interactive' organizations the interaction between the buyer and seller is relatively concentrated, with a focus on solving rather than identifying the client's problem. The emphasis is not so much on *what* customers want but on *how* to satisfy their wishes. For example, a client may require a new computerized payroll system but not possess the necessary know-how in-house to develop and install such a system. As

Mills and Margulies (1980: 263) write, 'the interaction, therefore, revolves around the task to be performed to a very considerable extent'. In these service organizations the interaction between buyer and seller is more complex, since it is based on a continuous and developing exchange between the two parties. This is necessary in order for the task to be completed.

The 'personal-interactive' type refers to organizations which focus on the personal problems of the service purchaser. The clients of these organizations 'are typically unaware or imprecise about both *what* will best serve their interest and *how* to go about remedying a situation' (Mills and Margulies, 1980: 264). Through interaction with the client the consultant seeks to generate information that can assist with the solution of the problem. The consultant aims to bring about an improved awareness in the client in order to make him or her more self-sufficient should the problem reoccur at some point in the future.

On the basis of this typology Mills and Margulies (1980: 263) suggest that the vast majority of business services are task-interactive organizations. This implies that they are primarily concerned with the provision of expert knowledge and information to solve problems originally identified by clients. However, in relation to management consultancy, the generality of their typology fails to capture the nuances of specific types of consultancy activity. For example, Schein (1969) distinguishes between the following models of consultancy:

1 The 'purchase of expertise model', in which the client first identifies the problem and then buys the required service. In this model consultancies act as task-interactive organizations.
2 The 'doctor–patient model' in which the client is uncertain as to the cause of a problem. A consultant is brought in to diagnose what is wrong and then to recommend a solution or prescribe a remedial measure. In this model consultancies act as personal-interactive organizations.
3 'Process consultation', in which the client and consultant work jointly at diagnosing the problem and developing a solution. The aim of the consultant 'is to pass on the skills of how to diagnose and fix organizational problems so that the client is more able to continue on his own to improve the organization'

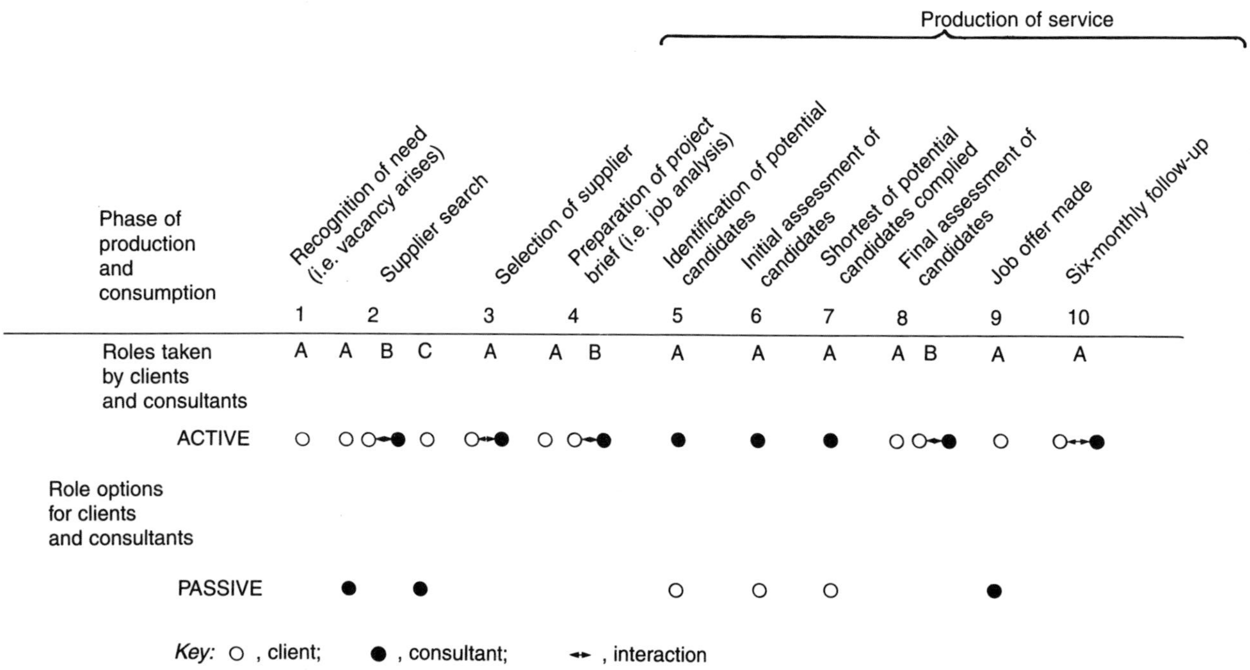

Production of service

Phase of production and consumption	1	2	3	4	5	6	7	8	9	10

1. Recognition of need (i.e. vacancy arises)
2. Supplier search
3. Selection of supplier
4. Preparation of project brief (i.e. job analysis)
5. Identification of potential candidates
6. Initial assessment of candidates
7. Shortest of potential candidates
8. Final assessment of candidates compiled
9. Job offer made
10. Six-monthly follow-up

Roles taken by clients and consultants

	1	2	3	4	5	6	7	8	9	10
	A	A B C	A	A B	A	A	A	A B	A	A

Role options for clients and consultants

ACTIVE

PASSIVE

Key: ○ , client; ● , consultant; ↔ , interaction

Figure 3.1 The nature of interaction during the production and consumption of an executive recruitment service
Source: based on O'Farrell and Moffat (1991: 212, Figure 1)

(Schein, 1969: 11). Hence, this type of consultancy is cyclical. Initially the consultancy works with the client in a personal-interactive mode. However, as the knowledge and self-sufficiency of the client grows, the client–consultant relationship becomes more and more task-interactive. Indeed, an explicit aim of this type of consultancy is to reduce the dependency of the client on the consultant. Empowering the client is at the core of this model of consultancy.

Schein's (1969) classificatory schema suggests that management consultancy services are not predominantly task-interactive, since the exchange between the client and consultant is not always focused on solving problems identified by the client.

A further problem with Mills and Margulies's (1980) three-fold typology is its failure to recognize that while direct interaction between the client and consultant is a central feature of services such as management consultancy, for without this there is no performance, each party may adopt different roles at various stages in the production and consumption process (O'Farrell and Moffat, 1991: 209). This suggests that while the client – consultant relationship develops within and is bounded by a particular consultancy assignment, direct interaction between the two parties may not be continuous but may be limited to specific episodes. These are often the critical points that determine whether a client evaluates a particular consultancy as a high or low quality operation. As examples of very different patterns of client – consultant interaction, consider the consultancy work of executive recruitment consultants and management gurus.

Figure 3.1 outlines the interaction process that comprises the production and consumption of an executive recruitment service. This shows that during the ten phases which embrace the creation of an executive recruitment service, the nature of client – consultant interaction may vary. In other words, during a number of the phases each party may adopt a variety of different roles. Depending on which role is taken, direct interaction between the client and consultant may or may not occur. These options relate not simply to whether the client and consultant interact but also to whether either party has an active or passive role during any one phase.

To illustrate these points consider the following example of an assignment in which a consultancy is given the task of finding a client a new chief executive. The consultancy process begins when the client recognizes the need, for whatever reason, to replace the current chief executive (phase 1). This service may be delivered internally by the personnel function or alternatively through a market transaction with an external consultancy. Having decided to purchase the service externally, the client then identifies potential suppliers (phase 2). This may occur in one of three ways. The actions of previous consultancies may be evaluated internally (option A). The role of the consultancy is passive since it is its previous work that is being scrutinized. Alternatively, the client may discuss its need directly with a number of consultancies (option B). The final option involves the client drawing up a shortlist independently of potential suppliers (option C).

In phase 3 a consultancy is selected. Where more than one consultancy is being considered this often involves a 'beauty parade' with each consultancy making a presentation to the client. Once the consultancy is selected the project brief (phase 4) is jointly determined (option A). In some circumstances this may be prepared wholly by the client, although with reference to a consultancy's special abilities as outlined in its bid documentation. The next three phases (5, 6 and 7) are generally conducted wholly by the consultant, although the client has a passive influence in that the consultant is working within the parameters established by the project brief. The final interviews with the shortlisted candidates (phase 8) are most commonly conducted by the client, although again in some cases these are a joint exercise. The job offer (phase 9) is usually made by the client. Often it will draw on information contained in the candidate profile written by the consultant before the shortlist is submitted. The final phase involves the client and consultant meeting several months after the appointed candidate has been in post to evaluate the success, or otherwise, of the assignment.

Figure 3.2 shows the interaction process that comprises the performance of a management guru. In contrast to executive recruitment consultancies, management gurus are in continuous interaction with their audience of managers. The role options

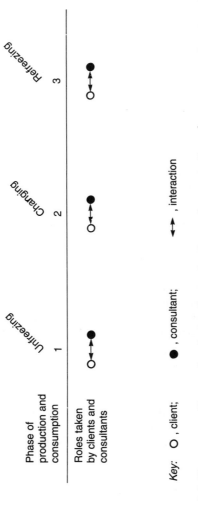

Figure 3.2 The nature of interaction during the production and consumption of a management guru performance
Source: based on O'Farrell and Moffat (1991: 212, Figure 1)

available to each party are therefore limited to direct, and active, interaction. This occurs since the focus of this type of consultancy activity is on the event itself and its subject is the managers present. The intervention activity largely takes the form of a verbal exchange in which the audience actively participate. Following Huczynski (1993: 250–67), Figure 3.2 distinguishes three phases to this type of consultancy work: unfreezing, changing and refreezing. In phase 1 (unfreezing) successful management gurus are

> able to induce some kind of nervous tension in their audience or stir up sufficient feelings of anger or anxiety, to secure potential converts' undivided attention, and possibly increase their level of suggestibility. The key here is to increase or prolong the stress in people, thereby altering their thinking processes, impairing their judgement, and increasing their openness to suggestibility.
>
> (Huczynski, 1993: 253).

Hence, the management guru initially establishes an atmosphere in which the emotional resilience of the participants is weakened, so that they become uncertain, self-questioning and anxious. The guru is then able to move on to the next phase (changing), in which the aim is to make the 'familiar strange by stepping outside of it', thereby 'disrupting the taken-for-grantedness of everyday life' (Mangham, 1978: 97) for the audience of managers. It is about restructuring the understandings of audience members so that they come to view the familiar in an unfamiliar but more enlightened way. As Burns (1992: 109) writes, 'before we can come to a fresh appreciation of what we experience, and, through that, actually come to *know* something instead of 'knowing *about*' it, we have to 'see with different eyes'. In the third and final phase (refreezing) these restructured categories are reinforced so that the old ways of thinking become supplanted by the new ones (Scheidel, 1967).

The discussion above has established that an essential feature of both these types of management consultancy activities is the collaboration or interaction between the client and consultant, although it may take different forms. As a consequence, the production functions of these management consultancy services are primarily relational in that they are based on the interaction between the client and consultant (Mills and Margulies, 1980: 260). Whether the outcome is considered a success depends not only on the performance of the consultant but also on how well the client and consultant interact. Therefore, a key objective for consultants is to manage and manipulate the interaction process in such a way that they convince clients of their value. Each episode of interaction provides consultants with an opportunity to convince clients that they have something special to offer. Indeed, the interaction process offers an opportunity for consultants to persuade clients of their special competence, expertise and skill. It is thus fruitful to see the work of management consultants as 'systems of persuasion' (Alvesson, 1993: 1011). We shall return to this point later in the chapter.

This highlights a further important distinction between goods and services, namely that there is often no separation between the consumption and production of services. Goods are produced, sold and then consumed. By comparison, services are sold and then produced and consumed simultaneously. Hence, the production and delivery of services are generally indistinguishable. In an executive recruitment assignment, for instance, the design of an advertisement or the production of a detailed profile of each candidate is the manufacturing process from the client's viewpoint. However, this is also the point at which the service is consumed from the consultant's viewpoint. If the delivery and, therefore, the consumption is poor, then the outcome of the consulting process, although it may be excellent, will be viewed as having been badly produced. Thus, in order for a consultant to meet a client's expectations he or she must effectively manage the simultaneity of production and consumption, i.e. the interaction process.

Heterogeneity

Heterogeneity refers to the extent to which services can be standardized. From the customer's point of view this specifically relates to consistent quality. Customers seek a high quality level of service each time a purchase is made. The degree to which services are heterogeneous depends on what can be termed their 'plasticity'. This refers to the amount of discretion available to a service provider when fulfilling the terms of a contract (Alchian and Woodward, 1988: 69). For instance, an ice cream vendor has little discretion when supplying its product to the public. Similarly, the ability of a computer software supplier to modify a particular package is limited by the original programmers' intentions, in addition to legal constraints. In contrast, management consultancies have considerable discretion since they are not selling a predefined package as in the other examples. Rather they are selling a bundle of services that can be modified and adapted in response to the idiosyncrasies of clients' problems and the interaction process. As Oberoi and Hales (1990: 702) write, 'This means that a service is unique to the consumers' requirements, and that standardization of service is difficult or impossible.'

Later chapters will suggest that this lack of standardization is a key contributor to the power and effect of certain consultant performances, such as those given by management gurus. In this sense these performances are managed events in which the consultant/performer consciously attempts to influence the response of other interactants (the clients or audience). The consultant/performer seeks to manipulate the situation for his or her own ends. To effect this, Goffman (1990) suggests, the actions contributing to and defining a performance tend to be idealized in that they conceal and underplay aspects which are inappropriate and therefore inconsistent with the impression that the management guru is seeking to generate in the audience. Furthermore, in order to relate more closely to an audience, performers may give the impression that the 'routine they are presently performing is their only routine or at least their most essential one' (Goffman, 1990: 56–7). To sustain this, Goffman suggests, a performer may use a number of techniques. One is to segregate the audience to ensure that different routines are not seen by the same individuals. For instance, an actor may maintain a screen persona that varies significantly from his or her roles in theatre. Another way of making an audience feel special is to foster the impression that a particular performance is unique. This is achieved by obscuring the routine features of a performance and emphasizing the spontaneous aspects. In addition, a performer may speak without notes, seek participation from the audience and personalize the presentation in some way (e.g. the inserting of the bride and groom's names during a wedding service, referring to a member of the audience by name), so as to convey the impression of spontaneity and uniqueness. This suggests that improvisation may be critical to the successful 'bringing off' of this type of consultancy work (Mangham, 1978).

The extent to which a service is heterogeneous may in part be determined by the way in which the two previous service characteristics – intangibility and interaction – are blended. For example, services that have a high intangible component and are produced in isolation from the consumer may be highly hetero-geneous since they are characterized by high 'plasticity'. Where these conditions prevail, the customer is unable to ascertain the characteristics of the service in advance of purchase and so is generally forced to rely on the seller's indications of the expected outcome. In essence, the customer is asked to buy a promise. Furthermore, where customers do not participate in the produc-tion of the service they are unable to determine the precise conditions under which the service was produced and, therefore, whether the seller took due care. Such circumstances can create an atmosphere of uncertainty between buyers and sellers.

In contrast, heterogeneity may be less prevalent in highly intangible services that are produced through a complex form of interaction. In such circumstances a customer may be able to impose a certain rigidity on the production and delivery of these services which minimizes the discretion of the service provider. However, this very interaction ensures that the service trans-action is a unique event. In other words, complex interaction ensures the heterogeneity of service delivery between service customers.

Perishability

Services are perishable, since they are destroyed in the process of consumption and cannot be stored. However, as in the case of intangibility, the distinction is not simply that services are perishable while goods are not. Some services are more perish-able than others. Greenfield (1966: 9), who introduced the

55

Table 3.1 Implications of service characteristics for management consultants and their clients

Service characteristics	Implications for management consultants	Implications for clients
Intangibility	Nothing to show clients *ex ante* except third-party reports, or direct experience of past services.	Quality difficult to determine *ex ante* and *ex post*.
	Impression management important since possibility of creating a reality which persuades clients of value and quality.	
Interaction	Outcome dependent upon quality of interaction with clients.	Outcome dependent upon quality of interaction with consultants.
	Management of interaction process offers possibility of convincing clients of value and quality.	Experience of interaction informs pre- and post-purchase evaluations of quality.
Heterogeneity	Considerable discretion over delivery of the service.	Quality difficult to determine *ex ante*. Quality variable.
Perishability	Service destroyed during consumption. Therefore difficult to replicate, hold stocks and expand output during periods of high demand.	Unable to purchase the same service.

concept of perishability in the context of business services, argued that much depended on the time span used to distinguish between perishable, semi-durable and durable. Commercial cleaning services, for example, may be classified as a perishable business service since the premises must be recleaned at regular intervals. Semi-durable services include advertising and marketing activities since these may undergo periodic review and change. Greenfield (1966: 9) classified durable business services as those concerned with the strategic direction of the firm, such as those provided by management consultancies, market research consultancies and R & D projects. These survive as long as they contribute to the strategic intentions of senior management. Furthermore, it is not necessarily the case that goods are more durable than services. A management consultancy report, a legal contract or a piece of music written by a composer may all have much longer lives than many so-called durable manufactured goods (e.g. confectionery, fuel, paper).

Implications for management consultants and their clients

From the above outline of the key characteristics that have been used by management scholars to differentiate between goods and services it is clear that they will have a significant impact on the way in which management consultancy services are delivered to clients. The following discussion seeks to ascertain the effects of the four service characteristics on the initial selection of a consultancy and the subsequent evaluation of the quality of the service once it has been delivered. Table 3.1 summarizes the key implications of these service characteristics for consultants and their clients.

In the management consultancy industry intangibility is a major source of quality assurance problems. This implies that services, such as management consultancy, are low in search qualities – attributes that can be ascertained prior to purchase (Nelson, 1970). Since services do not take on a complete physical form there is little that can be directly evaluated beforehand. Hence, ascertaining the quality of a consultancy's service at the pre-purchase stage is a major problem for clients, since whereas the supplier may know the level of service quality, the buyer often does not. This arises because clients are unable to observe and measure service quality at the outset and thereby distinguish between the relative quality of alternative consultancies. Since clients are incapable of sampling or testing a service prior to purchase, thereby determining its appropriateness, they are asked to buy what essentially amounts to a promise – a promise of a certain level of quality (Levitt, 1981: 96). This inability of clients to determine the characteristics of consultancies at the pre-purchase stage means that they have considerable difficulty in differentiating between high and low quality suppliers. In these circumstances clients will tend to view consultancies as perfectly substitutable since high and low quality suppliers appear identical.

The potential costs associated with this problem, where a seller's competencies are indistinguishable to a buyer, have been well described in Akerlof's (1970) study of the second-hand car market ('The market for "lemons"'). Consider the implications of Akerlof's model for management consultancy services. The ease of entry and high level of turbulence outlined in Chapter 2 implies that high and low quality consultancies will both operate in the management consultancy market place. Nayyar (1990: 514) notes that 'This coexistence requires buyers, *ex ante*, to determine the quality of goods and services they buy'. However, intangibility implies that the processing of information prior to purchase is inherently uncertain. Consultancies know their own abilities, while clients, because they are unable to verify the appropriateness of the service, are unable to distinguish between the relative qualities of alternative consultancies. Akerlof's (1970) model makes the assumption that if clients are unable to distinguish between the quality of consultancies they will view them as perfectly substitutable. As a consequence, *all* management consultancies will be able to charge the same fee. The high quality consultancies will not remain in the market since the fee they receive reflects that for the average quality of management consultancy services. Thus, they will be unable to reap the benefits from their 'competence enhancing investments' (Holmstrom, 1985: 188). Furthermore, the continued entry of poor quality consultancies will drive down the average industry price to reflect the deterioration in overall quality within the industry. High quality consultancies will therefore withdraw from the market place, further lowering the average level of service quality, the fee level will deteriorate and further attrition of high quality consultancies will occur. Where this occurs the market may degenerate to a point where only low quality consultancies exist. It must be stressed that this is a hypothetical example implied by Akerlof's model.

The intangibility of services also creates difficulties for clients when they come to evaluate the quality of the service they have received. If a service cannot be seen, touched, tasted, heard or smelled it is not sensitive to assessment by one of the five senses. Where intangibility prevails, judging the quality of a service is extremely difficult. However, as the earlier discussion of intangibility in this chapter indicated, services are rarely, if ever, completely intangible. Rather, services can be located on a continuum with the extremes of tangible and intangible. It was suggested earlier in the chapter that management consultancy is located towards the end of the intangible side of the scale. The great majority of services, management consultancy included, therefore contain, in varying degrees, some element of tangibility since they are invariably directed at tangible products. Purchasers are often able to evaluate the tangible component of the service. For example, bank staff work with money; mechanics work on car engines; and plumbers repair central heating systems. It is possible to examine a bank account to ascertain if any errors have been made. A car engine can be inspected to verify that a fault has been rectified. It is also possible to determine from the operation of a central heating system (i.e. the radiators are hot) whether or not it has been repaired.

However, evaluating a service which is predominantly intangible is more problematic since, as mentioned above, it may not be receptive to assessment by the five senses. Furthermore, to paraphrase Levitt (1981), intangibility implies that clients do not know what they have purchased until they get it. In these circumstances, according to Alvesson (1994: 544), clients rely on images or 'mental pictures of the phenomenon [i.e. service] concerned'. Since clients are not fully cognizant of the nature of the service they have purchased there is an opportunity for consultants to create and project a particular image of the service they are supplying by controlling and managing the way in which it is delivered (i.e. the interaction process). In other words, intangibility enables consultants to take command of the process by which images, impressions and perceptions of their value and service quality are created. Clients then use these tailored and controlled images as the basis on which to evaluate the value and quality of the service they have received. In this way consultants are able to convince clients that they are delivering a service which is both of value and high quality. The assignment process therefore allows the consultants ample opportunity to persuade clients of their high quality based on their special expertise, talents and skills. This implies that impression management is at the core of much consultancy work.

The ability of clients to assess the quality of services purchased is made more difficult, since, as Starbuck (1992: 731) notes, they

> often consult experts because they believe their own knowledge to be inadequate, so they cannot judge the experts' advice or reports mainly on substance. Clients may be unable to assess experts' advice by acting on it and watching the outcomes: the clients do not know what would have happened if they had acted otherwise and it is frequently obvious that outcomes reflect uncontrollable or unpredictable influences. Clients may not understand what their expert advisers are saying. Many experts – with awareness – use jargon that obscures their meaning.

As a result of these problems Starbuck argues that clients tend to make their judgements as to the value and quality of the service on the basis of 'generic symbols of expertise'. They therefore rely on signals or symbols of a supplier's competence and quality. These include the qualifications of the experts, the quality of data and use of impressive statistical computations, credibility of the analyses, and experts' dress, confidence and general demeanour. Hence, according to Starbuck (1992: 731), if we are truly to understand the success of management consultancies we must 'pay attention to their symbolic outputs'; that is, how they create impressions of their quality and convince clients of their value.

According to Jackall (1988: 132) management consultants are 'virtuousos in symbolic manipulation' (see also Bloomfield and Best, 1992; Bloomfield and Danieli, 1995).

The intangibility of services also implies that consultancies are unable to provide much in the way of tangible evidence to prospective clients of past performance, except verbal assurances, consultancy reports, testimonials from past clients and such like. This suggests that consultancies' promotional activities will concentrate less on advertising, direct mail and consumer guides and more on referral, word-of-mouth and repeat purchasing (Mitchell, 1994).

The characteristic of interaction suggests that management consultancy services are high in experience qualities – attributes that can only be discerned following purchase or consumption (Nelson, 1970). Like a bottle of wine, a restaurant meal or a book, the quality of a management consultancy service is determined during consumption. This indicates that the outcome of a consultancy service is highly dependent upon the quality of the interaction between client and consultant.

For clients this service characteristic reinforces the difficulty of identifying the quality of a management consultancy service prior to purchase. There is nothing to evaluate until the client and consultant interact to produce the service. This suggests that at the pre-purchase stage there will be a tendency for clients to emphasize the quality of interaction over other criteria. Hence, when choosing a supplier, clients are more likely to stress factors such as their, or others, previous experience with a particular consultant or consultancy in preference to factors such as fee levels, the quality of the written proposal and the size of a consultancy. This arises since it is the interaction between the client and consultant that creates the service. The collaboration, or interaction, between the two parties is the central and consistent feature of a consultancy service. This implies that a client's experience of this, and the way in which it is managed by the consultant, will be an important factor in the initial selection decision and subsequent evaluation of service quality. Quality assessment is therefore based on a client's experience of using a particular consultant or consultancy (i.e. their experience of the interaction process). In essence, clients make a judgement with regard to how they view their relationship with a particular supplier following a period of interaction. This evaluation then becomes a central feature of their information banks on different service suppliers.

This discussion suggests that when evaluating the quality of a service, pre or post-purchase, clients will tend to stress the quality of their experience with a particular supplier. This is based on the nature and quality of the interaction between the two parties. This means that in order to create the impression of a high quality service (i.e. to convince clients of their value), consultants must focus their efforts on the active management of the interaction process with clients. This emphasizes the importance of consultants managing the expectations and overall experience of the client in order to foster and convey the impression that they are delivering a high quality service. Alvesson (1993: 1011) argues that service organizations, such as management consultancies, are essentially 'systems of persuasion'. At the core of their work is the creation and management of impressions, i.e. convincing clients of their 'know how' and that they have something of value to offer. Indeed, he suggests that their rationale for existing and economic success are dependent upon the extent to which they are able to convince clients of their value.

The combined effects of the service characteristics of intangibility and interaction imply that clients base their evaluations of service quality on their experiences with particular suppliers. Good experiences lead to favourable evaluations. These in turn may increase the possibility of repeat business. Hence, consultants focus on the management of the interaction process in order to benefit from this state of affairs.

The characteristic of heterogeneity underpins the considerable variation in the delivery of management consultancy services. This stems largely from the central role that the client plays in the production and delivery of a consultancy service. Put simply, the interaction between clients and consultants ensures that no two assignments are the same. As a consequence each transaction between a client and consultant is unique. For consultants this leads to the possibility that each assignment represents a new start with a client. They are able to start again and use their considerable discretion to meet the particular requirements of each client and manage the interaction process so as to create further favourable evaluations of their service quality. This is possible since services are especially 'plastic' (Alchian and Woodward, 1988). That is, service suppliers have a high degree of discretion when fulfilling the terms of a contract; they are not constrained by a tight straight-jacket. They are free to tinker with, adjust and customize the various parts of the service they offer in order to meet the particular needs of each client and at the same time to convey the 'right' impression. This leads to the possibility that a highly individual and idiosyncratic service can be delivered in order to meet, and deal with, the particular requirements of each client. For executive recruitment consultants this could mean adopting little used selection techniques such as graphology (handwriting analysis). Management gurus may adjust different aspects of their consultancy work, such as the surroundings, the content, the duration of the event, their contact with the audience and so forth.

The creation and delivery of a very focused and individual service has different implications for consultants and clients. Linking this discussion to an earlier point, discretion enables management consultants to differentiate themselves from other suppliers. In having discretion over the way the contract is fulfilled they have an opportunity to manage the interaction process in such a way that a client is unable to obtain the same level of service elsewhere. The service they give, and have created for a particular client, is unique. For clients this implies that service quality may be variable. This arises for two reasons. First, if the delivery of a service is highly individualized it may not be appropriate for, or obtainable by, another client. Second, if a service cannot be repeated then indications of past performance may have little bearing on current or future delivery.

Conclusion

This chapter has argued that services differ from goods in a number of important respects. In particular, services are characterized by high levels of intangibility, interaction, heterogeneity and perishability. These service characteristics have a number of implications for the users and suppliers of management consultancy services. Intangibility suggests that purchasers will have difficulty selecting between alternative consultancies, since there is no material form that can be evaluated beforehand. Buyer's are therefore ill-informed about the relative quality of the alternatives they are considering. Indeed, they may view them as perfectly substitutable since high and low quality suppliers will appear identical.

Intangibility further implies that convincing clients of their worth is a vital part of consultants' work. The inability of clients to determine the quality of individual suppliers means that management consultancies must in some way convey to their clients that they have something valuable to offer. Because clients do not know what they are getting until they get it, consultants are able to take control of the process by which impressions and perceptions of service quality are created. Clients then use these carefully constructed 'images' when evaluating the quality of the service they have received. By managing the creation of these images, consultants are able to persuade clients of their value and quality. Impression management is therefore at the core of consultancy work.

This is further reinforced by the characteristic of interaction: production and consumption do not occur separately. Services are sold, and then produced and consumed simultaneously. This implies that at the pre-purchase stage there is nothing to evaluate until the client and consultant interact to produce the service. Furthermore, it suggests that the quality of what is produced, and therefore evaluated after delivery, is to a large extent dependent upon the outcome of the interaction between the client and consultant. Hence, clients are likely to place considerable stress on the quality of the interaction process when selecting between alternative consultancies. This means that clients will tend to emphasize evaluations of previous interactions, based on prior experience, when choosing a consultancy. Therefore, if consultants are to persuade clients of their quality, and convince them of their value, they must actively manage and manipulate the interaction process in order to create favourable impressions of their service. To be successful, management consultants must pay particular attention to this aspect of their work.

Their ability to do this is further enhanced by the heterogeneity of services. Consultants are not able to deliver a standardized service. While this might imply variable quality to clients it offers consultants the opportunity to tailor their services to the particular requirements of individual clients. They are able to modify the service they offer in order to meet the particular needs of each client and at the same time to convey the 'right' impression. Therefore, heterogeneity gives rise to the possibility that consultants are able to manage the interaction process in many and various ways. Thus, there are a wide range of devices, mechanisms and tools available to consultants seeking to create, manage and manipulate client impressions of their service.

Before examining how consultants seek to persuade clients that they have purchased a valuable and high-quality service, the next chapter focuses on how clients choose between different suppliers of management consultancy services at the pre-purchase stage.

4

CHOOSING A MANAGEMENT
CONSULTANT

―――――――――――

Introduction

Chapters 2 and 3 have highlighted the various ways in which the
structure and dynamics of the management consultancy market
and number of service characteristics impact on the client–
consultant relationship. Two problems in particular have been
noted. The first relates to the difficulty of assessing the quality of
a potential supplier prior to purchase. The second concerns the
difficulty of evaluating the quality and value of a service once it
has been delivered. The primary aim of this chapter is to identify
mechanisms which enable clients to overcome the problems
associated with the market features and service characteristics
elaborated earlier, and to choose a supplier they believe to be of
high quality. In other words it seeks to provide a tentative answer
to the first question originally posed in Chapter 1 – how do clients
choose a supplier of management consultancy services? Three
mechanisms are considered in detail: contingent fees, regulation
and reputation. The potential importance of these mechanisms
has been highlighted by a number of service industry commentators and researchers (see Holmstrom, 1985; Nayyar, 1990;
O'Farrell *et al.*, 1993). In addition, their possible significance is

reinforced by the interviews conducted with clients and consult-ants.

The subsequent discussion is structured around an evaluation of each of these mechanisms in terms of their ability to assist clients to determine the relative quality of different suppliers. Depending on their usefulness clients are more or less able to select a high quality supplier of management consultancy ser-vices.

Contingent fees

Within the management consultancy industry there are two general fees structures.

1 Time-based fees – clients are charged according to the amount of time the consultant works for the client. Consultant time is usually charged at a daily rate but, depending on the duration of the assignment, fees may also be charged by the hour, week or month.
2 Fixed fees – here the client and consultant agree a set fee for the assignment from the outset. This is negotiated according to the time, complexity and resources required. These fees may be calculated on either a contingency or a retainer basis. Contin-gency fees are dependent upon results, and according to Kubr (1986: 401), 'have one or both of the following characteristics: (1) the fee is paid only when specific results are achieved; and, (2) the size of the fee depends on the size of the results'.

Generally, contingency fees are rare in the management consultancy industry. However, the most common fee struc-ture in the executive recruitment industry displays the two features mentioned above. Consultancies are only paid on the successful completion of the assignment, that is when a candidate is employed by a client organization. The level of the fee is calculated as a percentage of the anticipated first year's remuneration package of the successful candidate (salary plus any guaranteed bonus, etc.). Such payments are either time or performance (i.e. partially contingent) related. In the first, clients are invoiced over specific periods of time, such as 30, 60 and 90 days. In the second, clients tend to pay at the commencement of an assignment, on submission of an acceptable shortlist and on the appointment of a shortlisted candidate. The third tranche is a contingency element dependent on a candidate being employed from the presented shortlist. However, whichever fee structure is used, in executive search the total cost of an assignment does not vary much between 30 and 33 per cent of the candidate's first year's remuneration package. In executive selection, fees range from 18 to 22 per cent of the appointee's guaranteed first year's remuneration package.

Consultancies that charge retainer fees are paid for their professional services for a specified period of time. Fees are never contingent on the success of an assignment. For example, a major source of income for management gurus is their personal appearance fees from presentations given at conferences and management seminars. They are paid for their attendance at these events and some are rumoured to earn as much as £20,000 per presentation.

Contingent fees may enable a client to identify a high quality service provider in a number of ways. Such fees may signal higher quality since a consultancy whose fee is dependent upon the successful outcome of an assignment has more confidence in its ability than one that does not want to take that risk. If a consultancy fails to deliver according to the terms of the contract the client may withhold a proportion of the total fee until the agreed service is fully delivered. This may necessitate the consultancy exerting considerable additional effort, which could have serious financial implications since consultancy staff may be diverted from other fee-earning opportunities. At the same time the tendency to oversell (i.e. to charge the client for services that are inessential) is reduced, since a consultancy's fee is dependent upon the outcome rather than the amount of time devoted to a particular assignment. A consultancy receives the same fee, excluding expenses, regardless of the effort exerted. In these circumstances there is a greater risk of a consultancy taking short-cuts in order to reduce the cost of conducting a particular assignment.

The contingent fee schedule may also motivate the consultancy to pay closer attention to the assignment so that the outcome is successful. If the intervention is deemed a failure a proportion of the fee is withheld. Therefore, contingent fees, in signalling competence and greater attentiveness, may partially reduce the informational gap (i.e. the inability of clients to distinguish high from low quality suppliers) between clients and the consultancies they are actively considering.

However, contingency fees may not be an effective way of signalling a consultancy's quality to potential clients for several reasons. First, research into the criteria used by clients to select consultancies repeatedly suggests that they emphasize other factors, such as the reputation of the consultancy and individual consultants. Fees do not appear to be a major factor when selecting a management consultancy. This is shown in Table 4.1, which summarizes the findings from four studies into the choice criteria used by clients when selecting different management consultancy services. Two of the surveys mention the cost of purchasing a consultancy service (Dawes *et al.*, 1992; Clark, 1993b). In both cases survey respondents rated it low on the list of factors influencing their choice of consultancy.

Second, as part of the wide-ranging interviews with 60 consultancies, interviewees were asked to identify the factors they believed accounted for their success at obtaining assignments. A content analysis of these answers is presented in Table 4.2. This shows that cost was the least mentioned factor along with the location of a consultancy.

Regulation

Given the difficulties associated with selecting a management consultancy and then evaluating the quality of the service once it has been delivered, it might be expected that the management consultancy industry would be formally regulated in order to ensure quality consistency. In particular, the characteristics of intangibility and perishability lead to problems of ensuring and monitoring quality. These characteristics imply that the delivery of a service is inherently uncertain. This problem is more acute in an industry where entry and exit barriers are low. In these

Table 4.1 Criteria used by clients to select consultancies: summary of evidence from four surveys

	Stock and Zinszer (1987) (logistics consultants)	Dawes et al. (1992) (management consultants)	Askvik (1992) (management consultants)	Clark (1993b) (Executive recruitment consultants)
1	Prior experience	Reputation of consultants	Reputation of consultancy	Reputation of consultants
2	Reputation of firm	General reputation	Prior experience with consultancy	Reputation of consultancy
3	Consultants who will work on project	Client knows specific consultant(s)	Prior knowledge of consultants	Knowledge of client
4	Reputation of consultants	Prior experience with consultancy	Reputation of consultant	Expertise
5	Ability to assist in implementation	Experience in client's industry	Personal recommendation	Personal recommendation
6	Other clients served	Prior experience of consultants	Academic background of consultant	Quality of formal presentation
7	Cost of services	Written proposal	Quality of formal presentation	Cost
8	Ability to help sell recommendations to top management	Consultant will assist with implementation	Approached by consultancy	Methods
9	Professional recognition of consultants	Cost of consultants	Quality of advertising	Location of consultancy
10	Availability of analytical techniques	Formal presentation	Completely arbitrary	Size of consultancy

Note: The first ten criteria from each study are listed in order of importance.

Table 4.2 Factors accounting for a consultancy's success in obtaining assignments

Factor	Percentage*
Existing relations with clients	93
Reputation of consultant	88
Reputation of consultancy	87
General image of quality	77
'Word-of-mouth' recommendation	72
Quality of presentations	58
Cost	45
Location	45

* More than one response was possible.

circumstances there is little collective control over the constitution and certification of industry participants. Rather the industry is a fragmented and diffuse collection of organizations, many of which choose to offer the service for monetary gain rather than through any commitment to a higher purpose (a professional ethic, client service, etc.). As a consequence, some consultancies may adopt a fly-by-night strategy in that they are here today and gone tomorrow. Such consultancies display little long-term commitment to the industry and by inference to their clients. Indeed, as the discussion in Chapter 2 showed, the industry is composed of a large number of transient firms, as demonstrated by the high level of turbulence. For some industry participants, management consultancy is something that they dabble with as long as profitable opportunities are perceived, for others it is a career stop-over while they are between jobs. The following quotations taken from a number of interviews with management consultants illustrate their short-term attitudes towards the industry:

I have been doing this for a couple of years now . . . quite honestly I can't see myself continuing much longer.

I live from assignment to assignment . . . so long as my clients want my services then I will continue.

I fell into management consultancy and could easily fall out.

According to Rashid (1988), it is in markets where entry barriers are low and turbulence high that quality has the greatest tendency to vary and potential to deteriorate. In such circumstances tight regulation might be expected in order to assist clients to distinguish between the relative qualities of the plethora of organizations offering management consultancy services.

Owing to the heterogeneity of organizations offering management consultancy services three sources of regulation can be distinguished: government-initiated codes, industry specific codes and non-industry specific codes. Each of these is considered in greater detail below.

Government-initiated codes

The discussion of barriers to entry in Chapter 2 indicated that there were no legal impediments to the establishment of a management consultancy. In general there is no legal framework which determines the constitution and certification of industry participants. However, consultancies that offer executive recruitment services currently have to be licensed in accordance with the provisions of the Employment Agencies Act (1973). This Act defines an employment agency as 'the business of providing services (whether by the provision of information or otherwise) for the purpose of finding workers employment with employers or of supplying employers with workers for employment by them.' This covers a wide range of activities, from office staff agencies, through entertainment and model agencies, to executive recruitment consultancies. As an employment agency activity, all organizations offering executive recruitment services are required to obtain an employment agency licence in accordance with the provisions of the Act. The application procedure is standardized and uncomplicated and the licence fee is inexpensive (£114) in comparison to the total cost of establishing a consultancy.[1] Furthermore, the act is not a 'primary' barrier to entry since there are no requisite pre-entry qualifications. Any person can establish an employment agency. The Act merely elaborates an application procedure and provides a minimum standard of behaviour.

72

Industry specific codes

These refer to codes that emanate from a variety of regulatory bodies within the management consultancy industry. Perhaps the two most well known of these bodies are the Management Consultancies Association (MCA) and the Institute of Management Consultants (IMC). Each of these regulates small segments of the industry. The 35 members of the MCA operate according to a code of professional conduct. This has five general rules, which cover: (a) the disclosure of confidential information obtained during the course of an assignment; (b) the taking on of work in areas where the consultancy is not competent; (c) the maintenance of objectivity and therefore a respectful distance from clients; (d) the terms of remuneration; and (e) behaviour likely to bring the industry into disrepute.

Similarly, the behaviour of the IMC's 3,500 members is regulated according to a code of professional conduct. This is founded on the following three general principles: (a) high standards of service to the client; (b) independence, objectivity and integrity; and (c) responsibility to the profession.

Non-industry specific codes

The discussion of entry into the management consultancy industry in Chapter 2 indicated that 27 per cent of interviewed consultancies were divisions of accountancy firms. As a consequence, the code of professional conduct for the Institute of Chartered Accountants in England and Wales (ICAEW) may be relevant to the activities of some consultants in some management consultancies. These rules are aimed at encompassing a wide range of activities and so do not relate specifically to the activities of management consultancies. Rather, the rules encompass management consultancy by default since some members of the ICAEW happen to offer these services.

The weakness of government regulations, the patchwork of management consultancy codes covering very specific and tightly defined areas of the industry and the low level of membership of industry bodies all suggest that these three sources of regulation generally fail to alleviate or circumvent information asymmetries in the management consultancy industry. Few clients are able to seek redress from an industry body. Evidence from interviews with both consultancies and clients suggests that when recourse is made to these codes of conduct the relationship between the two parties has already been irretrievably lost. Clients, rather than waiting to make a claim, more often than not transfer their allegiance to another consultancy. Such actions by clients indicate that they place little importance on these codes of conduct despite their potential as a source for indicating the quality of different management consultancy suppliers. Furthermore, as Tables 4.1 and 4.2 indicate, neither clients nor consultants consider regulation an important factor for differentiating between consultancies.

In summary, these three sources of regulation do not appear to offer much assistance to clients seeking to differentiate between the relative quality of alternative suppliers of management consultancy services.

Reputation

Tables 4.1 and 4.2 indicate that both clients and consultants report that the reputation of the consultancy and/or individual consultant is the most important factor for choosing between alternative management consultancies. Reputation may therefore be an important factor enabling clients to ascertain the quality of different service suppliers.

What is meant by reputation? According to Belkaoui and Pavlik (1991: 232), reputation is an 'important signal of a firm's organizational effectiveness'. O'Farrell *et al*. (1993: 45) write: 'reputation is often referred to as the goodwill value of the firm's name or loyal customer patronage.' Hence, a firm has a good reputation as long as buyers believe its services to be of a high quality. Therefore, it is the *buyers' perceptions* of the service that determine whether a supplier is characterized as the provider of high or low quality services, and hence whether it has a 'good' or 'bad' reputation. However, what are these perceptions based on when in service markets the characteristics of intangibility, interaction, heterogeneity and perishability imply that the quality of suppliers' services is difficult to ascertain prior to purchase? In these circumstances how do clients determine whether service suppliers have good or bad reputations? According to Levitt (1981: 96), 'when prospective customers can't experience the product in advance, they are asked to buy what are essentially promises.' Therefore, reputation is something to do with buyers' perceptions of the quality and trustworthiness of sellers' promises. Suppliers with good reputations tend to deliver the level of service they promise. In contrast, suppliers with poor reputations cannot be relied upon to deliver a consistent level of service; they tend to fail in some respect. There is therefore a greater likelihood of dissatisfaction and disappointment when using suppliers with poor reputations.

This discussion suggests that reputation is a type of signalling activity in which the quality of services delivered in past periods serves as a signal of the quality of those delivered in the current and future periods. Buyers use assessments of a seller's *past* performance as a way of forecasting future quality. In this way the development of a reputation is dynamic, since the benefits of past actions accrue in the future (Shapiro, 1983: 659). Consistently meeting past promises is viewed as a good indicator that future promises will also be kept. Suppliers are motivated to maintain the delivery of high quality services since they are concerned about the future demand for their services (Holmstrom, 1985: 189). If the quality of their service should slip then this will be deemed by potential purchasers as a break with the previous pattern and therefore a possible indication that future promises may not be kept. A supplier's reputation may suffer as a consequence.

Two types of reputation can be identified in the management consultancy industry: individual and corporate. The former relates to the reputation of individual consultants; the latter refers to the reputation of consultancies rather than their personnel. The interviews with clients in part sought to identify the key criteria which undergirded their assessment of these two types of reputation. The results are shown in Table 4.3. This indicates that 'past experience' with either the consultant or consultancy is the most important factor underpinning buyers' evaluation of reputation, followed by 'personal recommendation' and 'brand

Table 4.3 Sources of reputation in the management consultancy industry

Source of reputation	Percentage*
Past experience with consultant	92
Past experience with consultancy	84
Personal recommendation	48
General awareness/brand image	36

* Results based on content analysis of 25 interviews with users/buyers of management consultancy services; more than one response was possible.

name'. These findings suggest that clients obtain information on a supplier's past performance in two main ways. The first is through direct experience of a consultant or consultancy and may be termed *first-hand reputation*. The second is a more indirect route. Clients rely on the evaluations of others who may, or may not, have had direct experience of a consultant or consultancy. This may be termed *third-party reputation*. Each of these is considered in more detail below.

First-hand reputation

The importance of first-hand reputation supports Clark's (1993b: 245) observation that clients primarily evaluate reputation, 'in the main, in terms of a history of past transactions with individual consultants. Frequent transactions between consultants and clients leads to a familiarity which underpins the latter's assessment of the former.' The following quotations taken from the interviews with clients illustrate this.

X used to work here in the personnel department. He left to join a recruitment consultancy. Some time after he left a vacancy arose. We went externally and used X since he knew the type of person we wanted.

X worked for us some years ago.

When X moved consultancy we went with them.

We are a very individual company. This means few consultancies understand our special needs. We have used X for a
number of years . . . I believe he may have moved consultancies a number of times.

The message contained particularly in the last two quotations is
reinforced by a survey reported by Watson *et al.* (1990: 55). This
found that 83 per cent of management consultancy users would
follow the consultant were they to move to another firm. This
suggests that client companies in some instances may use the
information gathered from frequent exchanges with consultants
to assess their, and through them the consultancy's, abilities to
deliver a high quality service. Granovetter (1985) suggests four
advantages in using people from whom one has already bought
services in the past. First, it is cheap. Second, people trust their
own information which they know to be accurate. Third,
individuals with whom one has had a continuing relationship
have an economic interest in succeeding, so as not to jeopardize
future transactions. Fourth, continuing economic relations often
become suffused with a social content that carries strong expectations of trust and abstention from dishonest behaviour
(Williamson, 1975). Echoing these points Maister (1989) suggests
three reasons why existing clients represent a consultancy's most
probable, and possibly profitable, source of new business: (a) the
clients' trust and confidence has been established, which should
result in a higher probability of success in obtaining new
business; (b) marketing costs are lower since the consultancy
possesses detailed information on the client and its industry; (c)
'follow-on' work from existing clients is more profitable than
first-time engagements since the consultancy incurs minimal
set-up costs and is already advanced along the learning curve.

Experience of a particular supplier is not necessarily confined
to the management consultancy industry since reputation can be
transferred between a number of different service markets.
Chapter 2 indicated that a large number of management consultancies are already established firms in other industries (i.e.
cross-entrants). This suggests that consultancies may be able to
transfer their reputation from one industry to another. This is
recognized in Hines's (1957) definition of 'entry', which states

that a firm in one market may have such a strong reputation that the mere expression of an intention to expand into another market can produce defensive reactions from the existing or current group of industry participants. Thus, it is the contention of this book that the reputation requirements within the management consultancy industry are similar to those in several other industries. Hence, reputation within the management consultancy industry can be transferred to, and from, several closely related industries and services, which include, among others, accountancy, advertising and public relations.

However, in order for an organization effectively to confer its reputation to a number of different services within its portfolio of business activities, the transfer must be perceived as legitimate by buyers. As Nayyar (1990: 516) writes, 'Potential buyers must believe that the diversifying firm can and will deliver the expected quality in the new service.' For instance, it might be reasonable to expect that an accountancy firm, with its experience of management systems and the consultancy process, could claim to have the range of skills necessary to offer management consultancy services. In contrast, it is less likely that potential buyers will believe that the same firm is equally competent to operate a hotel, restaurant or airline. This occurs because the transferability of reputation between services is limited by the extent to which the reputational requirements of different services are similar. Buyer perceptions of quality differ between some services and are similar across others. Hence, reputation can be transferred between services where the experiential requirements which underpin evaluations of quality are similar. Where reputational prerequisites differ, inter-industry transfer is not possible. Given the earlier point that reputation is based upon the quality of past services, the successful completion of a management consultancy assignment does not inform the potential buyer whether the same organization could ensure a relaxing sojourn at a hotel, a delicious meal or a comfortable flight. In contrast, accounting, advertising or public relations skills may have direct relevance to management consultancy work. These parallel skills may include experience of winning assignments, defining the brief, organizational analysis, report writing and assisting with the implementation of recommendations.

Nayyar (1990: 516) further suggests that once a reputation has been acquired 'it can be used over and over again in the context of other services or markets.'[2] Every time a client company uses a seller's services these experiences are added to an information bank about the services it has used. When a known service provider (i.e. one with whom the buyer has some previous experience) introduces a new brand, 'buyers may draw upon their information banks to form associative evaluations of the likely properties of the new brand' (Nayyar, 1990: 516). Hence, buyers who have favourable experiences of a seller's existing service(s) may transfer these to the new service. Buyers may then favour these sellers over more established, but untested, service providers. For example, a buyer may prefer to purchase management consultancy services from its auditor rather than risk transacting with a specialist consultancy with whom it has no prior experience. In other words, there may be a tendency for buyers to limit their service purchases to a small number of diversified sellers. This implies that as long as the transfer of reputation is legitimate, sellers can offer a range of related services to existing and potential buyers. As a consequence, firms with strong reputations, and large client bases, may come to dominate a number of related service industries. This is undoubtedly the key factor underpinning the expansion of accountancy firms into the management consultancy industry. They are able to leverage their reputation in one or more services to establish strong client preferences for new, and as yet untested, services.

In summary, the fluidity of reputation between several related industries suggests that while first-hand reputation is an important factor determining the selection of particular consultancies by clients, it is not necessarily founded upon their management consultancy activities.

Third-party reputation

Tables 4.1 and 4.3 indicate that personal recommendation is an important factor used by clients to evaluate whether a consultancy can and will deliver the expected level of quality. This refers to recommendations from individuals who may, or may not, themselves have direct experience of a particular consultant or consultancy. In essence, buyers are using the information banks of other purchasers of management consultancy services to supplement their lack of knowledge. This is a form of 'social capital' in that buyers use their social relations with other buyers so that they may be able to select a management consultancy. Social capital therefore refers to social structures that limit the impact of the market features and service characteristics referred to in the previous chapters and enable transactions to occur that otherwise would not take place. Coleman (1988: 118) defines it as the knowledge which is 'embodied in relations among persons'. Examples of such networks of social relations include families, religious communities, clubs of all kinds, groups of friends and so forth. One example of the operation of social capital is in the wholesale diamond market. Coleman (1988: 98) writes:

> In the process of negotiating a sale, a merchant will hand over to another merchant a bag of stones for the latter to examine in private at his leisure, with no formal insurance that the latter will not substitute one or more inferior stones or a paste replica. The merchandise may be worth thousands, or hundreds of thousands, of dollars.

Given these circumstances, why does the buyer not cheat the diamond seller by either replacing or stealing the bag of stones in his or her temporary possession? What is it that makes this seemingly precarious and irrational transaction possible? Coleman suggests that the answer is 'social capital'. The strength of close family, community and religious ties ensures that the transaction can occur with ease for two reasons: (a) the fear of being ostracized from any one of these groups ensures that the buyer will act in a trustworthy manner towards the diamond seller; and (b) the frequency of interaction between the buyer and seller means that the former continually has an opportunity to evaluate the trustworthiness of the latter. Coleman (1988: 99) suggests that, 'In the absence of these ties, elaborate and expensive bonding and insurance devices would be necessary – or else the transaction could not take place.'

When choosing a management consultancy on the basis of personal recommendation, clients make an assessment of reputation on the basis of past dealings with trusted individuals rather than with the consultancy itself. Frequent exchanges between the members of networks, such as those mentioned above, enable them to make judgements as to the reliability and accuracy of information supplied by trusted informants. In other words, the *first-hand* reputation of these trusted informants is used as a proxy measure for the reputation of the supplier of management consultancy services. Therefore, the reputation of the seller is determined indirectly, via third-party recommendation. Our feelings as to the trustworthiness of the informant, based on our interaction with him or her, are projected on to the supplier. Thinking back to the example of the haircut used in the opening chapter, we may select a particular hairdresser because they are recommended by a member of our family or close personal friend. In doing this we use our perceptions of the trust-worthiness of their advice, derived from frequent interactions with them, as a way of determining the potential quality of the hairdresser's service. Indirect evaluations of a supplier's quality are the essence of third-party reputation.

Discussion

With first- and third-hand reputation identified as the most important criteria used by clients to select management consul-tancies, it remains to be ascertained whether there are any notable differences in emphasis between first-time (i.e. infre-quent) buyers and more experienced (i.e. frequent) users. Does the fact that a client has no previous experience of purchasing management consultancy services mean it ascertains the quality of potential suppliers in a different way from those who are more experienced? This question has been considered by Dawes *et al.* (1992), who found that less frequent buyers of management consultancy services place even greater emphasis on sources of information derived from existing social relations. Their research results suggest that information arising from existing social relations with suppliers and other purchasers is of greater importance to first-time buyers. In particular they:

- are more likely to select a consultancy with which they have had prior experience;

- place more importance on dealing with an individual consultant whom they know personally;
- rely more heavily on personal recommendation.

In summary, these findings, in conjunction with the previous discussion, indicate that buyers of management consultancy services, whether frequent or infrequent, generally choose between alternative suppliers on the basis of their reputation. A supplier's reputation is based upon buyers' perceptions of the quality of services delivered in past periods. The past is used as an indicator of the future. These perceptions of service quality are primarily based on either a buyer's direct experience of a particular supplier or recommendations from third parties. In both instances the formation of reputation is 'embedded in concrete, ongoing systems of social relations' (Granovetter, 1992: 32). First-hand reputation arises from direct interaction between buyers and sellers, whereas third-party reputation is derived from the social relations between buyers. This suggests that reputation in the management consultancy industry is socially constructed. It is dependent upon the development of perceptions of quality that arise from past and continuing interaction between the different parties to the transaction.

The previous discussion suggests that the dominant transaction in the management consultancy industry is the relational exchange. This arises since these transactions are not short-lived *ad hoc* arrangements but unfold and develop over a long period of time (Macneil, 1980). Indeed, the relationship between buyers and sellers is open-ended in that it has no foreseeable end. This longevity is founded upon an evolving relationship arising from the repeated social interaction between the two parties. Each period of interaction forms part of the transaction history between the two parties, as well as ensuring that the relationship continues into the future. Therefore, each transaction 'must be viewed in terms of its history and its anticipated future' (Dwyer *et al.*, 1987: 12). As a consequence, there are two features to each relational exchange. The first aspect has already been discussed in some detail and relates to the history of past transactions between buyers and sellers. In essence, buyers (i.e. clients) use their evaluations of previous interactions with particular sellers

(i.e. accountancy firms, advertising agencies, management consultancies) as a way of choosing *ex ante* between alternative
service providers. These information banks underlie buyers'
perceptions of a seller's quality. Second, each transaction acts as a
basis for securing the future collaboration between the two
parties. The success of an assignment lies in the extent to which
consultants are able to manage the interaction process in such a
way that clients accept the 'image' of the service that is created
and presented to them. Consultants have to convince clients of
their unique value and quality thus making themselves indispen-
sable (Callon, 1986; Law, 1992). If this were not the case buyers
would be able to transfer their purchases between sellers, thus
undermining the continuous and long-term nature of the transactional relationship. Were this to occur exchanges between a
buyer and its supplier(s) would gradually become characterized
as discrete transactions.

In contrast, discrete transactions refer to transactions between
buyers and sellers as conceived by classical and neo-classical
economics, in that they deny 'any impact of social structure or
relations on production, distribution, or consumption. In competitive markets, no producer or consumer noticeably influences
aggregate supply or demand or, therefore, prices or other terms
of trade' (Granovetter, 1992: 29). Furthermore, Macneil (1980: 15)
writes that 'Everything about the discrete transaction is short –
the agreement process, the time between agreement and performance, and the performance itself. The discrete transaction
commences sharply by clear, instantaneous agreement and
terminates sharply by instantaneous performance; sharp in,
sharp out.' There is therefore no presumption that a buyer will
enter into a further exchange with a particular seller at some point
in the future. The only obligation that exists between the two
parties is that the buyer will purchase a good or service from a
seller at a specified price. Nothing exists to inhibit a buyer
subsequently transferring its patronage to another seller. In
discrete transactions a buyer will enter into an exchange with one
seller on one occasion, with another on another occasion and so
on, depending on who charges the lowest price. The buyer is not
concerned about who fulfils the contract. The focus is on the
substance of the exchange, rather than with any concern for

future relations and exchanges. They are 'here-and-now' transactions 'segregated in time and space from other transactions' (Arndt, 1979: 70).

The point being developed here is that the nature of relational exchanges means that each assignment provides consultants with an opportunity to project their special and distinctive competences to clients by 'bringing home' distant events, places and people. This is achieved by: (a) rendering them *mobile* so that they can be brought back; (b) keeping them *stable* so that they can be moved back and forth without additional distortion; and (c) making them *combinable* so that they can be cumulated, aggregated and manipulated (Latour, 1987: 223). Legge (1994: 3) writes that this is precisely what management consultants do 'when they make the experience of (distant) forms accessible and combinable through the development of (in Latour's terms) equations or packages – such as McKinnsey's decentralization package, HAY-MSL's job evaluation package or even Peter's eight rules of excellence.' But she also notes that in order for these packages to achieve marketability and impact they need to be made credible to existing and potential clients. She identifies this issue as critical to the work of consultants. Understanding how consultants achieve impact is the focus of the next two chapters.

Conclusion

This chapter has sought to identify the mechanisms that enable clients to overcome the uncertainties created by the market features and service characteristics elaborated in previous chapters, and to choose a supplier that they believe to be of high quality. It has sought to answer the first question originally posed in the introductory chapter: how do clients choose a supplier of management consultancy services? Three mechanisms were considered: contingent fees, regulation and reputation. The ensuing discussion suggested that contingent fees are not a useful way of determining a supplier's quality since price is not an important criterion for clients when choosing between consultancies. Furthermore, formal regulatory mechanisms are weak.

Government-initiated codes are virtually non-existent and therefore offer little protection for clients. The same point applies to industry-initiated codes, in that these encompass a small percentage of organizations operating within the industry. As a result of these deficiencies there is no industry-wide body which determines the competence of individual suppliers.

It was suggested that clients choose suppliers of management consultancy services on the basis of their reputation. This refers to a client's perception of a supplier's quality based upon evaluations of its past performance. These evaluations are socially constructed in that they are dependent upon ongoing relationships with suppliers and other users of management consultancy services. In the first instance assessments of a particular supplier's quality are derived from direct experience of that supplier. This is termed *first-hand reputation*. In the other instance clients rely on the assessments made by other users of consultancy services whom they trust. This is termed *third-party reputation*. Therefore, clients use evaluations of previous interactions with suppliers of management consultancy services, based on direct experience and third-party reports, to ascertain quality *ex ante*.

This chapter has therefore argued that clients choose between the suppliers of management consultancy services on the basis of their evaluations of the quality of services produced in past periods. These evaluations are ascertained via social relations with suppliers and users of management consultancy services. These social relations can be characterized as relational exchanges. These have two important features. First, parties choose to liaise with each other on the basis of their evaluations of past episodes of interaction. Second, each period of interaction influences whether the parties will interact at some point in the future. Since suppliers of management consultancy services are chosen by clients on the basis of past and repeated experiences of the interaction process, consultants must carefully manage this in order to convince existing and potential clients of their continuing value and quality. The next chapter begins to explore how we might best understand how they achieve this.

5

THE DRAMATURGICAL
METAPHOR

Introduction

Chapter 4 argued that at the pre-purchase stage clients primarily choose between alternative suppliers of management consultancy services on the basis of first-hand and third-party reputation. They use evaluations of previous interactions with suppliers, based on either direct experience or third-party reports, to ascertain the quality of a supplier's service prior to purchase. However, it is still not clear what users of management consultancy services are evaluating in order to differentiate between high and low quality service suppliers. What are their evaluations of service quality based on? Put differently, what is it that the suppliers of management consultancy services are doing to enhance their reputations and increase the likelihood of future transactions? In essence, how are consultants managing and manipulating the interaction process so as to create the impression that they are delivering a high quality service which is valued by their clients?

The purpose of this chapter is to suggest that in order to answer these questions the most appropriate way of understanding and analysing the activities and work of management consultants is in terms of the theatrical analogy or dramaturgical metaphor. The author and Graeme Salaman have examined the dramaturgical nature of consultancy work and the advantages of using this metaphor for understanding the client–consultant relationship in a number of papers (Clark and Salaman, 1993, 1994, 1995a, b, c). The discussion in this chapter and the next uses and draws on the ideas presented in these publications. A major advantage of this metaphor is that it highlights the key features of what happens when clients and consultants meet and 'work' together. The main strength of this metaphor is that it emphasizes the nature of client–consultant interaction and draws attention to the fact that, and the ways in which, this is manipulated by the consultants in order to convey an impression of value and quality to clients. The most useful metaphor with which to view the activity and work of consultants is therefore one that focuses on consultants' attempts to create and manage meaning within the client–consultant relationship. It must capture how consultants seek to demonstrate their expertise, value and quality to clients when services are intangible, results are difficult for clients to evaluate, there is no obvious knowledge base on which to do this and there is enormous competition from other suppliers.

This chapter argues that the key to an understanding of consultancy and its success is to appreciate that successful consultancy in its methods, at least, recognizes, and indeed emphasizes, this aspect of client–consultant relations. In this respect consultancy work can usefully be understood in terms of the general rubric of theatre. Consultants seek to create and sustain a reality that persuades clients of their value in the same way that actors seek to create a 'theatrical reality'. Therefore, the principles of theatre – actions, setting, scripts, etc. – undergird the way in which consultants seek to manage their relationships with clients and the way in which we come to comprehend this.

In seeking to apply the central features of this metaphor to the activities of management consultants the chapter is structured in the following manner. Initially the previous literature that has sought to categorize the work of management consultants in terms of a variety of roles, styles and metaphors is critically examined. This is followed by a discussion of the nature of metaphor. Finally, the chapter explores the key features of the dramaturgical metaphor. The approach taken, although eclectic, is primarily derived from a number of key writers in the 'dramaturgical school'. Specifically, the view of performance propounded in the last part of the chapter derives from the writings of Kenneth Burke, Erving Goffman and Iain Mangham.

Current metaphors of the client–consultant relationship

Before we explore and develop the notion of consultancy work as a dramatic event, it is useful to examine, albeit briefly, the previous literature that has sought to conceive the activities of consultants in terms of a variety of roles, styles or metaphors. One of the earliest classifications was proposed by Tilles (1961) who, distinguished between three roles: seller of services, supplier of information and business doctor dispensing cures. The first is regarded by those involved in terms of a conventional sales-purchase transaction; the second in terms of the flow of information between the parties; the third in terms of patient and doctor. As mentioned in an earlier chapter, Schein (1969: 5–12) distinguished between three types of consultancy, which differ according to the roles of the consultant and client and the type of assistance sought, these are the purchase of expertise, doctor–patient and process models. Building on this classification, Margulies and Raia (1972) developed a model that locates the consultant's role along a continuum, with the extremes of task orientation and process orientation. At the former end of the scale the consultant is a technical expert, developing, recommending and implementing solutions to identified problems. In contrast, at the other extreme the consultant is a process facilitator working with the client in a collaborative manner so as to facilitate client learning in order to improve problem-solving processes within the organization.

More briefly, Steele (1975) identified nine roles that the consultant may adopt within a client system: teacher, student, detective, barbarian, clock, monitor, talisman, advocate and ritual pig. Ganesh (1978) identified and elaborated two distinct consultancy styles: the human and systematic relations orientations. The former emphasizes personal, interpersonal or subsystem issues, while the latter is concerned with task, structure and total organization environment issues. Lippitt and Lippitt (1979) developed a descriptive model that presents the consultant's role along a continuum, with the two polar extremes of directive and non-directive. As consultants become less and less directive, they suggest, their role undergoes a number of changes that occur in the following sequence: advocate to informational expert to trainer educator to joint problem solver to alternative identifier and linker to fact finder to process consultant and finally, at the other extreme, to objective observer/reflecter. Sinha (1979) produced an edited collection in which consultants use some of these roles to reflect on their own styles and approaches to consultancy. Blake and Mouton (1983: 14) identified five 'consulting modes', which differ in terms of the way the consultant relates to the client, i.e. in terms of theories and principles, prescription, confrontation, catalytic and acceptant. Nees and Greiner (1985: 69–70) identified and discussed the implications of five types of management consultant: mental adventurer, navigators, management physicians, systems architects, and friendly co-pilots.

A major deficiency with much of this literature is its grounding in a root or structural metaphor of the consultant as professional helper. In part this may arise since many of these commentators are, or were at one time, active and highly successful consultants. The consultancy roles they seek to identify are therefore based in large part on their own activities and reflect their conceptualizations and understandings of their own consultancy activities and the reasons for their success. In general, they appear to view their activities as synonymous, if not coterminous with, the role of professional helpers remedying illnesses, in this case of an organizational variety. Consequently, many of the consultancy roles identified above seek to highlight and reinforce professional status and professional autonomy, as well as assuming a major and acknowledged body of specialist knowledge. Therefore, these commentators invariably seek to impose and perpetuate a conception of the consultant role and function in terms analogous to the activities of a doctor, lawyer, therapist or other professional activity. In view of this focus there are three main deficiencies with the way in which the work of consultants and their relationships with clients have previously been understood and conceptualized.

First, many of them emphasize precisely what is *missing* from the relationship between client and consultant – an agreed, accepted, authoritative and relevant body of knowledge in which the consultant is accomplished and expert, but which is denied to the client and can be used as a basis on which to build the client–consultant relationship. A number of commentators have noted that while there is consultancy knowledge that is deployed during the consultancy activity, it lacks the status and authority of other professional knowledge and so does not supply a basis for occupational qualification and certification (see Whiteley, 1989; Oakley, 1993). This arises because management consultants have failed to establish control over a distinctive domain of knowledge. Rather, the management consultancy industry is characterized by a plethora of 'distinctive' bodies of knowledge. These include, among many others, organizational development (OD) models, or such models as the Boston Consulting Group matrix, transactional analysis, learning models, Gestalt theory and role theory. The very variety and diversity of these models and frameworks, which are the knowledge base of consultancy work, demonstrates that knowledge in the industry is actively contested.

This fluidity in the knowledge base of management consultancy is demonstrated by the consultant-driven, package-led, orientation of certain types of consultancy work. Parts of the consultancy industry are to some extent fashion-led, faddish and ephemeral. This is recognized by Gill and Whittle (1992), who argue that management consultants tend to peddle the latest in a long line of panaceas targeted at organizational improvement. Witness the emergence, initial enthusiasm, spectacular growth and then decline in popularity of such consultancy movements as conglomeration, intrapreneuring, the managerial grid, management by objectives (MBO), management by walking about (MBWA), organizational development (OD), T-groups and total quality management (TQM). The inherent cyclicality of such panaceas has the dual effect of expanding the knowledge base of consultancy work while at the same time destabilizing and then refocusing the activities of many consultants as they seek to 'climb aboard' the latest fad.

Perhaps the readiness of many management consultants to adopt the latest panacea demonstrates the inherent weakness and fragility of much consultancy knowledge. Alternatively it may reflect a common desire and eagerness among today's managers for the instant solution or 'quick fix'. Many managers appear to be in search of the 'holy grail', that vital piece of knowledge which will lead to organizational success and ultimate stardom. As Byrne (1986: 47) has noted:

> Today, the bewildering array of fads pose far more serious diversions and distractions from the complex task of running a company. Too many modern managers are compulsive dieters: trying the latest craze for a few days, then moving restlessly on.

Pascale (1991: 19) argued that management ideas 'began to acquire the velocity of fads after World War II'. He attributes this to the ascendancy of *professional management*, which was based on the premise that 'a set of generic concepts underlies managerial activity anywhere'. This assumption of universality meant that 'new' management ideas and techniques, as they were developed, could be marketed and disseminated very widely and quickly. They could be packaged and marketed like any other global product.

Whatever the reasons underlying the faddish nature of much modern management thought, consultants have played an important part in perpetuating and proselytizing many of these ideas. The amorphous knowledge base of the management consultancy industry has expanded and contracted to adapt to the shifting sands of modern management ideas.

In the absence of a clearly delineated and defended formal body of knowledge, consultants' success is determined by their ability to appear authoritative via their manipulation of a knowledge base that is ambiguous, tacit and constantly under threat. In the face of competing knowledge bases consultants have to appear authoritative by convincing prospective clients that their expertise is worth buying. Therefore, their skill lies in presenting themselves as experts and convincing clients that they provide the most relevant solution. They must persuade clients of their definition of the situation and persuade them to collaborate on the basis of this analysis. The creation, management and regulation of impressions and images is therefore a central feature of consultancy work. It becomes necessary for management consultants to draw upon various symbolic resources in order to convince clients of their inherent worth: their expertise, skills and talents. Through their actions consultants must generate images that are sympathetically received by clients, and lead them to value the service being offered and recognize its quality. Thus, impression management is a central feature of consultancy work.

Second, these images of the client–consultant relationship are excessively embedded in a focus on the rationality of modern organizations and modern industrial society. The metaphors assume the same 'celebration of rationality' within organizations as noted by Weber. 'When Weber wanted to contrast the organizations of industrial capitalism with those of other civilizations he identified their most distinguished characteristic as a belief that their affairs were conducted legally, reliably, consistently, calculatingly, and predictably, magic having been banished from their procedures' (Turner, 1990: 83). The views of the consultants' work and relationships mentioned earlier draw upon the same rationalistic, utilitarian, formalistic, hard-headed assumptions. Yet the actual nature and focus of much consultancy work deliberately opposes these values, and succeeds because of it. This point will be developed further below.

Third, the distinguishing qualities of the client–consultant relationship lie less in the currently available metaphors for institutionalized/professionalized assistance, counselling or exchange, and more in the *nature of the interaction between these two parties*. While supporting the value of metaphorical conceptualizations of the relationship between the parties (although wishing to move beyond the rational, secular, industrial context used by most commentators), any useful metaphor will capture the key features of what actually happens when clients and consultants meet and 'work' together.

This point needs emphasizing. The critical feature of consultancy that must be captured and highlighted by a metaphoric understanding is systematically overlooked by the majority of metaphors currently in use, since these over-stress the knowledge and professionalism elements of the consultancy activity and underestimate the role of client–consultant interaction. Oddly, despite the considerable emphasis in the OD literature of the importance of process in the consultants' task (e.g. Schein, 1969), relatively little attention has been paid to examining and understanding the dynamics of client–consultant interaction. Yet this interaction is critical. Following Legge (1994), the key question to ask of consultancy is not 'What is consultancy knowledge?' but 'How do consultants develop a "strong story"?' That is, how do consultants convince clients that they are authoritative, competent, expert, knowledgeable, skilled and can deliver a quality service? Legge (1994: 4) identifies a number of rhetorical techniques that consultants may employ: 'this involves developing a package that is self-fortifying and well positioned, i.e., a product that not only clearly identifies its potential clients but which anticipates and answers their potential objections to the claims made in an on-going fashion.' She notes that this involves linking claims to statements that the client already believes, arranging statements hierarchically so that they support each other: manipulating the client to arrive at a conclusion that he or she has already identified.

Attention to the processes whereby consultants demonstrate their value to clients is necessary since, as was noted earlier, their value does not reside in the knowledge base of the activity. Oakley (1993) has usefully noted that a distinguishing feature of consultancy is that, unlike in a profession, people cannot become qualified as consultants through 'rigorous and long training that leads to certification or licensure' (Blau, 1984; quoted in Oakley 1993: 4). The point is not that such training is unavailable but that it is irrelevant, as the key to consultancy success lies more in the *consultancy activity as a process of construction of meaning and impression management* than in the mastery of any esoteric theory that might underlie it. Oakley (1993: 6) notes that one of the characteristics of 'knowledge industries', such as management consultancy, is that the knowledge which underlies success 'resists complete codification of a formal kind but . . . is dependent on the appreciation of complex relationships and the practice of craft skills embedded in systematic, reflective understanding.'

Therefore, the focus of consultants' efforts must be to overcome the inherent limitations of the activity. Great efforts must be made in order to persuade clients of their authority, expertise and quality. It is thus fruitful to see consultancy work as symbolic action. Our metaphors of their work and their role must focus on how they make their claim to be of value clear, credible and distinctive. Our metaphors of their work must acknowledge their use of metaphors with their clients, i.e. their construction of myths and meanings by a process of persuasion. They must recognize that 'knowledge is inseparable from the rhetorics of persuasion and hence in a real sense [management consultancies] . . . might be seen, *par excellence*, as "systems of persuasion"' (Legge, 1994: 6). It is not surprising therefore that consultants have been regarded as 'merchants of meaning' using 'labels' to introduce order and certainty, by giving a name to things, while metaphor 'breaks through old labels, creating a hope for change, for something new'; for while 'labels say what things are, metaphors say what they are like and could be like' (Czarniawska-Joerges, 1990: 144–5).

To overcome the criticisms outlined above the remainder of this chapter argues that the distinguishing qualities of the client–consultant relationship lie less in the currently available metaphors for institutionalized/professionalized assistance, counselling or exchange, and more in the nature of the interaction between these two parties. These existing metaphors of consultancy work fail to turn 'imagination in ways that forge an equivalence or identity between separate elements of experience . . . creat[ing] meaning by understanding one phenomenon through another in a way that encourages us to understand what is common' (Morgan, 1983: 602). Indeed, the conventional metaphors of the client–consultant relationship not only fail to 'turn imagination', they suppress and obstruct the illumination and understanding of each party's role. If a major objective of much consultancy work is to manage client impressions, then similarly our understanding of how this is achieved may need to be supported by a drastic revolution in *our* taken-for-granted conceptions of the consultant's role. *Our* metaphors of *their* work should allow us to illuminate their work by transforming it, just as they seek to illuminate and transform the work of their clients in order to improve organizational effectiveness.

So far in this chapter there has been a great deal of 'talk' about metaphor, but what is it and is any one metaphor, such as the dramaturgical metaphor, better than another? The next section considers these two questions.

The nature of metaphor

Ortony (1975) has remarked that metaphors are necessary, not just nice. This implies that any understanding of the world in general is inherently metaphorical. In this sense, our theories and explanations of social and organizational life are underpinned by metaphorical structuring. Similarly, Morgan (1986: 12) argues that 'the use of metaphor implies *a way of thinking* and *a way of seeing* that pervade how we understand our world generally.' Metaphor is essential to our everyday language, thinking and expressive abilities, for 'our conceptual system, in terms of which we both think and act, is fundamentally metaphorical in nature...the way we think, what we experience, and what we do every day is very much a matter of metaphor' (Lakoff and Johnson, 1980: 3).

This argument is hardly new. For instance, Stephen Pepper in his book *World Hypotheses* (1942) argued that Western philosophers organize their knowledge of the world in terms of four world hypotheses (formism, mechanism, contextualism, organicism) and that each of these is generated and determined by a separate *root metaphor* (similarity, machine, historic event, integration). Pepper argued that the world hypotheses are complete and coherent world-views, in that they can 'handle fairly adequately any fact that is presented to them' (p. 98). World hypotheses are therefore all-encompassing in their explanatory scope. Each has a similar degree of exegetic power, but draws attention to, and therefore obscures, certain features of the social world. In other words each world hypothesis is equally capable of explaining the world in general, *but in its own terms*.

More recently, Gareth Morgan (1980, 1986) has examined the way in which organization theory is imprisoned by its metaphors. He develops a hierarchical link between 'paradigms', 'metaphors' and 'puzzle-solving activities'. Building on the work of Kuhn (1970), he suggests that organizational studies is

95

comprised of a number of paradigms or 'schools of thought'. These are distinctive ways of seeing the world and are therefore alternative views of social reality. As with Pepper's world hypotheses, each paradigm is a relatively coherent system of ideas based on a shared metaphor. The relevant research areas and methods (i.e. puzzles and puzzle-solving activities) are suggested by the metaphorical imagery underpinning a particular school of thought. As Morgan (1980: 611) writes, 'The use of a metaphor serves to generate an image for studying a subject. The image can provide the basis for detailed scientific research based upon attempts to discover the extent to which features of the metaphor are found in the subject of inquiry.'

Metaphor is used whenever we understand and experience one thing in terms of another. Thus, metaphor proceeds from the assertion that A is (or is like) B, where A and B were previously classified and understood as different entities. This combination or juxtaposition of A and B creates new meaning which is absent until the two elements are joined. As Schön (1979: 259) writes, 'It is the restructuring of the perception of the phenomenon named by "A" and "B" which enables us to call "metaphor" what we might otherwise have called "mistake".'

An important feature of metaphor is its selective focus. Metaphor highlights certain aspects of a phenomenon and hides others. When we comprehend one phenomenon in terms of another we tend to develop a lopsided understanding. In highlighting certain features metaphor forces others into the background, or even conceals them altogether. As Ortony (1979: 6) writes, 'metaphors result in a sort of cognitive myopia, in which some aspects of a situation are unwittingly(?) emphasized at the expense of other, possibly equally important, ones.' For example, we might describe an athlete as being 'like a leopard on the track'. In choosing the term 'leopard' we draw attention to, and conjure up, specific images of an animal moving with explosive speed, power, strength and grace. At the same time this metaphor requires that the athlete possesses selected features of a leopard. We ignore the fact that a leopard is a wild animal with feline features, yellow and black spotted fur, four legs, claws and a tail. Instead we concentrate on those features that the athlete and leopard have in common. In this way metaphor presents a partial truth. It gives a distorted image in which certain aspects of the phenomenon are included while others are excluded. Metaphorical comparison is therefore necessarily selective.

As is the nature of any metaphor the dramaturgical metaphor is a selective and compact image in that it draws attention to specific properties of consultancy work. In the argument that consultancy is a dramatic event in organizational life, those features associated with other metaphors of consultancy, such as 'consultant as advocate/lawyer' or 'consultant as evangelist', are forced into a background role. When the dramaturgical metaphor is emphasized certain features of consultancy are highlighted while others are hidden. When we use the theatrical metaphor we might think of the consultant as an 'actor', performing to an 'audience' in an 'improvised' manner according to a number of 'script headings', while utilizing 'props' and 'cues' in an organizational 'setting'. By way of contrast, when a consultant is likened to an advocate/lawyer we might focus on the consultant as a 'professional' with 'technical expertise', working to a 'brief' from a client when arguing a 'case' in front of a 'judge and jury'. When we think of a consultant as an evangelist our attention turns to religious imagery. A consultant may be viewed as a 'guru' who 'preaches' a message from a 'divine text' to 'followers' and potential 'converts' who then 'sign up'. In this sense the consultancy market is comprised of a number of competing 'sects'.

However, a critical feature of the dramaturgical metaphor is its broad scope. Its boundaries are wide enough to incorporate the imagery associated with the other two metaphors. Both the 'consultant as advocate/lawyer' and 'consultant as evangelist' metaphors can be incorporated within the dramaturgical metaphor. Each of these metaphors is inherently theatrical. Thus, a lawyer performs to a brief (script) in a courthouse (stage/setting), to a judge and jury (audience), using 'cues' from witnesses and pieces of evidence (props). Similarly, an evangelist's performances are tempered by their interpretation of a religious text (script), often delivered from a pulpit in a church (stage) to followers and churchgoers (audience), to the accompaniment of music and the singing of hymns (props). Furthermore, both of these performances are conceived and prepared in a private space prior to enactment in front of an audience. In this respect, just as the images of 'machine' and 'organism' are structural metaphors in organization studies (Morgan, 1980), the dramaturgical metaphor may be considered the primary metaphor for understanding the nature of consultancy work. The next section discusses the central features of the dramaturgical metaphor as propounded by Kenneth Burke, Erving Goffman and Iain Mangham.

The dramaturgical metaphor

Previous commentators have largely ignored the extent to which organizations – and the consultancy activities that contribute to, and benefit from, organizational life – are replete with their own 'ceremonies, rites and drama' (Turner, 1990: 85). This section will argue that the key to an understanding of the activities of management consultant is to appreciate that when successful they, in their methods at least, recognize, and indeed emphasize, this aspect of client–consultant relations. In this respect the work of management consultants is inherently theatrical.

In seeking to examine the work of consultants in terms of the dramaturgical metaphor, we focus on what happens when clients and consultants meet, or more particularly on how the consultant manages the client's perceptions of the event. Essentially, as Levitt (1981) has dryly noted, clients are asked to 'buy a promise'. What are the circumstances under which this 'promise' is offered, believed, sold? More specifically, following Burke (1945) the question becomes how can we explain the act of consultancy in terms of his five 'generating principles': act, scene, agent, agency and purpose. Any complete account of social behaviour, he argues, will 'offer some kind of answer to these five questions: what was done (act), when or where it was done (scene), who did it (agent), how he did it (agency) and why (purpose)' (Burke, 1945: xv).

There are two useful features to Burke's approach. First, the focus is on how we can understand other's actions. The focus is on *action*, on understanding what *actually happens* when people interact. Burke (1945: xvii) attempts to answer two questions: 'What is involved when we say what people are doing and why they are doing it.' Therefore, his interest is in seeking to understand how people interpret and make sense of their social world. He argues that when people seek answers to these questions they perceive, interpret and describe the behaviour of others in theatrical terms. For Burke it is inevitable that people come to understand their social world by employing the principles of drama, since human behaviour is inherently theatrical. When we engage in social intercourse 'we each know and understand each other's actions because each of us has to *act them out* or dramatize them' (Perinbanayagam, 1974: 536). In other words, we employ the principles on which we base our own social action in order to understand the social behaviour of others. So, as people engage in social action, they come to conclusions on the aforementioned questions, and are forced to do so, by the employment of dramatic principles. In this sense drama is not a mere analogy for social action – it is at the very heart of its generation and interpretation. The principles of theatre – words, actions, settings, scripts, scenes, cues, props, etc. – underpin our interaction with other people and the way in which we come to understand this. In this way, social action is generated within the same constraints as drama. Hence, to use Burke's terminology, the grammar of drama is also the grammar of social intercourse. Second, Burke describes his approach as 'dramatism' since it focuses on the 'intentions and purposes we read into other's actions, *as if we were members of a critically aware theatre audience*' (Burns, 1992: 109; emphasis added). Thus, Burke draws attention to the value of the dramaturgical metaphor for understanding organizational events, the value of regarding social action as if it were a theatrical performance.

Others have looked at theatricality in social and organizational life. Perhaps the most influential work in the dramaturgical analysis of social action is Erving Goffman's *The Presentation of Self in Everyday Life,* (1990; first published in 1959). In this he seeks to understand everyday social life and social intercourse in terms of the crafting of theatrical performances. His approach is openly theatrical. As he states in the Preface:

The perspective employed in this report is that of the theatrical performance; the principles derived are dramaturgical ones. I shall consider the way in which the individual . . . presents himself and his activity to others, the ways in which he guides and controls the impression they form of him, and the kinds of things he may or may not do while sustaining his performance before them.

(Goffman, 1990: 9).

By pursuing the dramaturgical metaphor beyond the commonplace notion of 'putting on an act' he creates an analytical structure which compresses Burke's dramaturgical Pentad (act, scene, agent, agency and purpose) into two basic notions: (a) performances must be addressed to an audience, and the part played by the audience is critical; and (b) any performance is comprised of two regions, a 'front-stage' and a 'back-stage'.

Goffman (1990: 32) defines a performance as 'all the activity of an individual which occurs during a period marked by his continuous presence before a particular set of observers and which has some influence on the observers.' Any performance is a 'dramatic realization' in which the performer seeks to convey a certain impression in order to evoke a certain response from the audience. In this sense a performance is a managed event in which the performer consciously attempts to influence the response of the audience. Goffman's social actor is not determined and controlled by circumstances and the situation but seeks to determine and control. As he writes,

Regardless of the particular objective which the individual has in mind and of his motive for having this objective, it will be in his interests to control the conduct of the others, especially their responsive treatment of him. This control is achieved largely by influencing the definition of the situation which the others come to formulate, and he can influence this definition by expressing himself in such a way as to give them the kind of impression that will lead them to act voluntarily in accordance with his own plan.

(Goffman 1990: 15).

Thus Goffman draws attention to the creation and management of impressions as an important element in the successful 'bringing-off' of consultancy work. However, this does not imply that consultants deliberately seek to exploit and manipulate impressions since, as Mangham (1978: 28) notes, 'for the most part interaction proceeds smoothly on the basis that most parties to it are "unconscious" or only dimly "conscious" of their parts in creating, sustaining, and transforming impressions. Interaction, in many circumstances, has the quality of naturalness, a "world-taken-for-granted" that would be the envy of many a stage actor seeking to present "reality".' If this were not the case, according to Biddle and Thomas (1966),

> The dramaturgical model, for instance, may easily go beyond the plausible implication that some behaviour is intentionally engaged in to foster given impressions and to achieve instrumental objectives, generally, to the extreme view that all human encounter is fraught with self-interest, calculation, manipulation, deception, guile, deceit and suspicion.
>
> (Quoted by Mangham, 1978: 28)

The point being developed here is not that individuals seek actively to manipulate and cheat those with whom they interact, since they are equally capable of compassion, truth and love. Rather, whatever the intentions of the individual, whether these are perceived as positive or negative, they are at the centre of events as a creative and adaptive social being rather than as a puppet. In other words, each interaction offers the opportunity for an individual to mould the situation to his or her own ends, whether these are viewed as positive or negative.

The second feature of Goffman's dramatistic schema is the distinction between the 'front-stage' and 'back-stage' activity of every performance. The 'front-stage' region refers to that part of the performance which is visible, and at which the audience is present. This is the permanent, or fixed, part of an individual's performance, which defines the situation for the audience. Burns (1992: 112) notes that 'some time and space [is needed] for the preparation of procedures, disguises or materials, essential to the performance, or for the concealment of aspects of the performance which might either discredit it or be somehow discordant with it.' This is the 'back-stage' region. In this region the audience

101

is excluded, enabling the performer to relax 'drop his front, forgo speaking his lines, and step out of character' (Goffman, 1990: 115). The conduct of any performance is therefore characterized by a considerable degree of risk, danger and uncertainty. Should the veil drop and the 'back-stage' be revealed to the audience, the performer is exposed, with the consequence that the audience may reconceptualize the role of the performer.[1] Hence, all performances involve risk, since a crack may appear at any moment, which permits the audience a glimpse of the back-stage. To use a theatrical example, there is a constant danger that the scenery may collapse at any time to reveal the back-stage crew working the pulleys, trap-doors and other mechanisms that are used to maintain a sense of reality and the quality of naturalness. This point suggests that a key aspect of successful consultancy work is the successful management of risk, promise and opportunity within a particularly highly demanding situation that carries the potential of total and public failure or acclaim.

More recently, Mangham (1978, 1986, 1987, 1990; Mangham and Overington, 1983, 1987), building on the writings of Burke and his followers, has argued that life is not *like* theatre, but *is* theatre. For instance, in arguing that management is a performing art he compares an organizational performance by Lee Iacocca, President of Chrysler, with a theatrical performance of *Richard III* by the nineteenth century actor Edmund Kean and concludes: 'I am not arguing that Iacocca's performance is *like* a performance of Edmund Kean. I am claiming that it *is* isomorphic: his performing, like yours or mine *is* theatre' (Mangham, 1990: 107). For Mangham, then, we are all performers 'strutting' on different stages, whether we are actors in the theatre, politicians in the House of Commons, lecturers in a university, managers in a work organization or consumers on a shopping trip. In each case the individual is a performer preparing, rehearsing and then presenting a character to an audience with the assistance of props and cues. Furthermore, each one of us plays a number of different characters and roles in a variety of settings. If we were to think of our working day we might begin in the domestic setting as 'father', 'mother', 'child'; when at work we take on the role of 'manager'; at lunch when eating at a restaurant we become a 'customer', and so forth. This is similar to

Goffman's view of the individual as an institution managing a whole set of roles and social selves. According to Burns (1992: 107), Goffman presents the individual as 'a series of selves, one "inside" the other, after the fashion of a Chinese box, or Russian doll. There is an inner self lurking inside the self which is present, or presented, to the outside world of others.' This division of selves contains the possibility that during a social encounter an individual may function as playwright, director, audience and critic (Lyman and Scott, 1975: 106–11; Mangham, 1978: 27). As playwright the individual fashions a script, thus determining the overall purpose of the social encounter in addition to how this is achieved. As director, an individual assists both in the initial construction and interpretation of the roles that the players will act and in orchestrating the nature of their interaction (i.e. the movement of the actors on stage), thus constraining the responsiveness of the other actors. As an audience an individual is aware of the performances given by others, while as a critic he or she monitors and evaluates these.

In applying the theatrical analogy to organizational life Mangham (1978: 25) argues that 'The dramaturgical model of man is based upon the idea that man improvises his performance within the often very broad limits set by the scripts his society makes available to him.' This definition emphasizes two central features of any dramaturgical model of social action: *script* and *improvisation*. Much of what passes as everyday social intercourse, he argues, regardless of the context, is structured around the interplay between three different types of scripts: *situational*, *personal* and *strategic*. The first two concepts are derived from Schank and Abelson (1977: 61–6), who define a situational script as

> a structure that describes appropriate sequences of events in a particular context. A script is made up of slots and requirements about what can fill those slots . . . Scripts handle stylised everyday situations. They are not subject to much change, nor do they provide the apparatus for handling totally novel situations. Thus, a script is a predetermined, stereotyped sequence of actions that defines a well-known situation.
>
> (Schank and Abelson, 1977: 41)

They occur when the situation is clearly specified, where several actors have interlocking roles to follow, and where each of the actors shares an understanding of what is supposed to happen. Thus, actors 'assume and enact relatively clearly defined roles within the confines of the anticipated sequence of events' (Mangham, 1978: 34). For instance, in the classroom script there are the roles of teachers and pupils. The key script headings for a typical day at school may include the taking of the register of attendance, lessons, break, lessons, lunch, lessons, extra-curricular activities and homework. Whether in the setting of the classroom, the home or the working environment, Mangham argues, we are all acting out a number of familiar parts in a series of situational scripts.

When a performance is constructed to achieve some personal goal the actor is following a personal script. A personal script generally exists solely in the mind of its initiator. Unlike with situational scripts, the actors may not share an understanding of what is supposed to happen. In such instances, the actors who are being duped may be unaware that they are participating in a personal script and therefore have little cognizance of the role they are playing. Such scripts may be played out by confidence tricksters, fraudsters, con artists and so forth. However, there are a number of personal scripts that are common enough for them to have become stylized events. Examples include the performance of a second-hand car salesman, insurance salesmen, a jealous spouse, the circumlocutory politician and so forth.

The last type of script is termed a strategic script. This refers to a performance where the actor is seeking to initiate certain behaviours from those with whom he or she is interacting. These are particularly manipulative in that the performer is only too well aware of what he or she is trying to achieve. The actor consciously attempts to influence the response of others by planning and then invoking a strategic script. Such performances differ from personal scripts in that the actor is pursuing a private agenda rather than a personal goal. Examples include a manager attempting to persuade colleagues, a therapist questioning patients, etc.

In developing the concept of a strategic script, Mangham (1978: 28) is seeking to emphasize the 'creation and management of impressions as an important feature of social interaction'. This view of performance has its conceptual roots in Goffman's version of the dramaturgical metaphor elaborated earlier. Implicit within this conception of performance is the idea that social actors, consciously or unconsciously, seek to create, sustain and transform impressions. For both Mangham and Goffman, therefore, a central feature of the dramaturgical metaphor is the art of impression management.

Mangham (1978) argues that improvisation is also critical to the achievement of any performance. A script is a 'detailed set of instructions for putting on a performance' (Cole, 1975: 6) and as such does no more than inform actors of the parts they are to play, their lines and their relationships to the other actors. While a script is the basis for a performance, it 'has nothing more than potential: the performer's text is an abbreviated and necessarily incomplete version of a possible work of art' (Mangham, 1990: 107). Similarly, Jenkins (1970: 205) writes that 'The performer's text is an abbreviated and abstract version of the real work of art, as this has been felt by the artist who created it, and the performer must give it the finished and concrete form in which it can be felt by an audience.' Hence, the task of the performer is to bring this text to full realization. This is achieved through a process that begins with the actor studying (i.e. 'reading') the text. On the basis of this, and perhaps also the influence of experience, fellow actors, the director and the expectations of the audience, he or she arrives at an interpretation which, through a process of trial and error during rehearsal, becomes embodied in actions on the stage. Jenkins (1970: 205) highlights two significant features of this process. First, a performance is a process in 'which meanings that are only implicit in the performer's text are made explicit in his performance'. In other words, the mysteries of the script are rendered intelligible to the audience by being embodied in the actions of the performer. Second, 'the performer must respect and realize the unique content and meaning of his text – of the work of art he is performing – but at the same time he must translate and embody this uniqueness in terms that are general and familiar, in order to make it publicly accessible and meaningful.' Thus, a performer, through his or her actions, must transform the unfamiliar into the familiar so that the interpretation has meaning for the audience to which the actions are addressed.

Cole (1975) has similarly argued that theatrical performances are concerned with making the script real, or to use his term 'present', for the audience. He does this with reference to the activities of shamans and hungans.[2] Both are concerned with accessing the supernatural, or what Cole terms the *illud tempus*. This refers to 'a time of origins, the period of Creation and just after, when gods walked the earth, men visited the sky, and the great archetypal events of myth – war in heaven, battles with monsters, the Quest, the Flood, the Fall – took place' (Cole, 1975: 7). Both these religious practitioners are able to make the *illud tempus* present again. This is accessed through trance by shamans and through possession by hungans. Cole suggests that a performance has both shamanistic and hunganic aspects, in that these are two successive stages in encountering the script/text (i.e. the *illud tempus*). He writes that 'The actor-as-shaman is the audience's envoy to the *illud tempus* of the script . . . The actor-as-hungan is the script's envoy to the audience' (Cole, 1975: 14–15). Linking this to the previous discussion, the performer-as-shaman is the reader and interpreter of the script (i.e. actor in rehearsal), whereas the actor on stage is the performer-as-hungan. In Goffman's (1990) terms performer-as-shaman is a back-stage, preparatory, activity whereas performer-as-hungan is front-stage, necessarily involving the audience.

In summary, what is meant when we say that the work of management consultants is inherently theatrical (i.e. dramatic). The basic elements of the dramaturgical metaphor suggested by the writings of Burke, Goffman and Mangham are presented in Table 5.1. Burke emphasizes the value of seeing and understanding all kinds of social interaction in terms of the dramaturgical metaphor. His approach therefore suggests that the work of consultants is not *like a dramatic event* but *is a dramatic event* in so far as they seek to use dramatic principles in order to create a reality that persuades clients of their value and quality. Burke's 'dramatism' thus encourages us to examine and understand the activities of management consultants in the same way we would any theatrical event. It transforms us from members of a passive puppet-like audience reacting to cues from those 'on stage', into

Table 5.1 The key elements of the dramaturgical metaphor

	The nature of performance
Burke	Social action is inherently dramatic.
	Act, scene.
Goffman	Audience.
	'Back-stage' and 'front-stage'.
Mangham	Script (situational, personal, strategic).
	Improvisation.

theatre critics seeking to comprehend and evaluate the performance we have just experienced. Rather than accepting the
outward appearance of social action, Burke encourages us to go
'back-stage' and examine the motives underlying social performances in greater detail, by utilizing a framework that reflects how
they are constructed in the first place.

While we concur with Goffman's definition of performance,
there is a need to go beyond this more explicitly. He defines
performance in terms of the presence of an individual before a
group of observers that has an impact on the observers. In doing
so he draws attention to techniques used by performers, as well
as the features of a dramatic performance, that enable a social
actor to create, transform and maintain impressions. These
include the performer's appearance, general demeanour and
manner in addition to his or her 'back-stage' preparation and
'front-stage' realization. Mangham builds on this view of performance by suggesting that if we are fully to appreciate how
performances are achieved, structured and realized then account
must be taken of the types of *script* in use and the way in which
actors *improvise* within a broad set of script headings (i.e. employ
personal and strategic scripts within the confines of a situational
script). In emphasizing these two features of performance
Mangham seeks to highlight the active role of the audience (i.e.
the other interactants or Goffman's observers) in the creation and
achievement of any social performance. For Goffman, while the
role of the audience is important it is there to be controlled and
manipulated by the performer. By defining the situation, a

performer is able successfully to 'convey an impression to others which it is in his interests to convey' (Goffman, 1990: 16). Mangham argues that this is too simplistic a view of interaction. He suggests that in reality all interactants are performers seeking to bring into play *personal* and *strategic* scripts within the general framework established by a *situational* script. He emphasizes the way in which 'meanings, identities, definitions, purposes and intentions . . . are modified by negotiation and through inter- action' (Mangham, 1978: 27). Thus, while both parties seek to exploit and manipulate impressions, interaction, for the most part, proceeds on the basis of negotiation and compromise. It is not a one-sided process.

The discussion in Chapter 3 noted that management consul- tancy services are highly intangible. Since clients are not aware of what they have purchased until they receive it, there is an opportunity for consultants to create a reality that structures the way in which clients evaluate the value and quality of the service delivered. This implies that clients invariably determine the quality of management consultancy services in terms of the 'images' created by the consultant. These 'images' result from careful management of the interaction process by the consultant. In these circumstances Goffman's view of performance seems most relevant. Consultants seek to manipulate the consultancy script (a situational script) by bringing into play their personal and strategic scripts and so ensure that these create a dominant and carefully structured and controlled image of the service they deliver.

Conclusion

This chapter has sought to argue that the most appropriate metaphor for understanding and analysing the work and role of management consultants is one which emphasizes the inter- action process with clients. In contrast, existing metaphors view the role and work of consultants in terms of a professional helper. In doing so they stress precisely what is absent from the client–consultant relationship: an agreed, accepted and authori- tative body of knowledge. However, management consultants have not been able to establish monopoly control over, and defend, a particular domain of knowledge. Rather, knowledge in the management consultancy industry is contested. In these circumstances consultants have to convince clients of their worth, and persuade them of their value, by creating positive images of the service they offer. Thus, impression management is a core feature of consultancy work.

The dramaturgical metaphor is primarily concerned with highlighting the theatrical/dramatic features of consultancy work. Its selective focus leads us to examine what happens when clients and consultants interact and 'work' together, and how this meeting is managed. It turns us into a critically aware theatre audience eager to understand and deconstruct the performance we have just witnessed. At the same time it provides a number of clear reference points to which we can attach our critical curiosity. Following the work of Goffman, this chapter has sought to indicate that when the dramaturgical metaphor is deployed the 'back-stage' and 'front-stage' aspects of consultancy work are highlighted. Furthermore, Goffman's social actor is not a puppet but a puppeteer. His social actor seeks actively to control and manipulate the impressions of the audience to which his or her actions are addressed. Indeed, impression management is at the heart of social intercourse. Similarly, Mangham stresses the way in which social actors seek to create, manage, sustain and transform impressions by structuring interaction around a number of scripts (i.e. personal and strategic). Social action proceeds on the basis of improvisation and negotiation as each party to an interaction episode seeks to exploit the situation for his or her own purposes by bringing into play personal and strategic scripts. The next chapter seeks to apply the dramaturgical metaphor to the activities of executive search consultants and management gurus in order to illuminate how these consultants create impressions of their service by controlling and managing client–consultant interaction.

6

CONSULTANCY AS
IMPRESSION MANAGEMENT

Introduction

The discussion in the previous chapter established that the dramaturgical metaphor offers new insights into the work of management consultants. Indeed, it offers a way of seeing that contrasts sharply with currently available images of their activities. These invariably conceive the consultant role in terms of a professional helper. Instead of the work of consultants being viewed as providing professional assistance with the diagnosis and curing of organizational ailments on the basis of a defined, defended and formal body of knowledge, this new metaphor focuses on their attempts to convince clients of their value and quality. In the face of strong competition and a weak knowledge base they must persuade clients that their service is worth buying. When seen through these new lenses a core feature of consultancy work is the art of impression management.

It was established in earlier chapters that consultants are able to manage the interaction process because of the intangible nature of consultancy services. Consultancy work is one of the most intangible parts of the service sector. Until the service is produced it only has potential. Indeed, it remains just a promise. With little in the way of tangible evidence to assess prior to purchase clients are forced to evaluate the value and quality of management consultancy services in terms of perceptions that result from their interaction with consultants. Since intangibility further implies that clients do not know what they are purchasing until they receive it, there is plenty of scope for consultants to create and convey, via their interaction with clients, a controlled and tailored image of the service they are delivering. Furthermore, the heterogeneity of services enables them to tailor their image creation activities to the particular requirements, peculiarities and needs of each client. Thus, it is by managing the interaction process with clients that consultants are able to build their personal characters or reputations. How is this achieved? Part of the answer has been provided by the discussion in Chapter 5 which emphasized the use of a number of theatrical devices (appearance, manner, 'back-stage', 'front-stage', scripts, improvisation, etc.). But how are these mechanisms used in practice so that clients are persuaded of a consultant's special competence and value? What is it that consultants actually do in order to manage clients' impressions of their service?

The purpose of this chapter is to answer these questions by examining two types of consultancy activity: executive search (colloquially known as headhunting) and management gurus. The aim of applying the metaphor to such diverse types of consultancy work is to demonstrate the inherent flexibility of this metaphor in that it is relevant to a wide range of consultancy activities. These applications of the metaphor have also been described in other writings (Clark and Salaman, 1995a, b).

Executive search consultants

The role of executive search consultants is to find suitable and appropriate candidates for senior level organizational roles. Sears (1982) concluded that executive search is the most common recruitment method at boardroom level. A survey conducted by Hoggett Bowers (1987) reported that executive search was the most favoured technique for recruiting staff earning more than £50,000. More recently, Clark and Mabey (1994) concluded that these consultants are primarily used to identify directors and specialist staff. In other words, executive search consultants are used to target a candidate population that is small, (usually no more than 50 persons) and difficult to access either because candidates are unlikely to respond to an advertisement or there is need for considerable discretion. The latter may arise for a number of reasons, such as that the organization does not want to signal its move into new markets to competitors, there are implications for the share price or the incumbent may be unaware that a replacement is being sought.

The assignment process outlined in Figure 3.1 can ostensibly be viewed in terms of the production and delivery of a purely rational and clear-cut service. In this sense executive search consultants seek to communicate job opportunities directly to potential candidates who may be suitable and interested in the vacancy. These are identified from three information sources: (a) networks of contacts; (b) databases which can comprise many thousands of names; and (c) original research – most consultancies have a team of researchers who can be deployed to conduct a detailed investigation of the relevant area. Following an initial contact, usually via the telephone, candidates are screened and interviewed, with those who are considered to have the greatest potential being presented to the client. The client then chooses from among the shortlisted candidates.

Clark and Clark (1990) have argued that these recruitment services do not simply provide a superior package to the identification, screening and selection services available within client organizations. Although these consultants may argue that their skills and knowledge result in the identification and recruitment of better quality candidates, as the following quotations taken from interviews with executive search consultants show, they offer an alternative rather than superior service.

When we take on an assignment we are not simply looking for candidates which fit the job description in the client brief. What our clients want is the outstanding candidate; somebody who will be a surprise to them. Our task is to find that person.

You live or die on the basis of the quality of the shortlist.

When we search we are trying to identify all the candidates who may be relevant to the client. We begin by locating where they might be. This hitlist is then shown to the client who is kept informed of our progress throughout the assignment. In this way there should be no surprises when the client meets the candidates.

This arises because executive search consultants have, in general, not developed their recruitment techniques beyond the capabilities of the in-house personnel function. They use similar selection techniques, primarily the unstructured interview and references, and the same professional recruitment model (see Wood, 1986) as the in-house personnel function. In other words, at first appearance these consultants do not appear to offer anything different from what can generally be obtained from in-house resources. The reasons for the increasing use of executive search consultants must therefore lie elsewhere. It is the contention of this book that the recent growth in the use of executive search consultants is linked to their skills as impresarios to the key event: the meeting of the sponsors and backers (i.e. the clients) with potential members of the cast (i.e. the candidates). Consultants are able to convince clients of their value and quality by effectively managing the 'back-stage' processes that lead up to this crucial event.

Hence, the activities of executive search consultants are focused in the main on managing the key event: the meeting between the client and candidates. This can be likened to an audition in that it is a crucial, fleeting performance where would-be members of the cast have an opportunity to display their qualities, supported behind the scenes by the advice and instruction of the executive search consultant. During the audition the candidates display themselves in terms of the roles and characters required by the selectors, showing mastery of themselves under trying and unfamiliar conditions, mastery of the situation and most importantly mastery of the organization they aspire to join: mastery, in short, of a script they have not been allowed to see but must infer competently and thoroughly. Candidates must show that they always wanted to play Hamlet, and are wonderfully prepared to do so; but the final qualification is that they know the script for a *Hamlet* which has never been written but is simply daily enacted, largely unknowingly, by the selectors. They are assessed as much for their knowledge of a script that does not exist as for their masterful performance of the script. Hence, what emerges during the interview is not tightly scripted or thoroughly rehearsed. Rather it replicates the process by which the organization script is developed and enacted. Following Mangham (1986: 64) 'it is more of an improvisation around a *scenario*'. The scenario (i.e. the interview) provides a broad framework within which the improvisation will occur. What emerges is therefore very dependent upon the actions of the performer. The competent candidate will have some general familiarity with the organization routines that underpin the scene; he or she will have related work experience and may even have considerable experience of selection interviews. The situation can be likened to someone entering a particular restaurant for the first time. On the basis of past experience they will have some idea of what to expect. However, their expectations, and accordingly their behaviour, will have to be modified depending on whether it is a 'sit down' or self-service restaurant. Furthermore, any unfamiliarity, and concomitant anxiety, with the scene is further reduced by the actions of the restaurant staff and the setting, which both give clues as to what behaviour is appropriate. For instance, a waiter sits a customer at a table with a menu and then returns, asking if the customer is ready to order. In a self-service restaurant signs often indicate where customers are meant to queue and menus are displayed in such a way that they facilitate meal selection by all customers.

However, unlike diners, candidates are attending a selection interview; it is a test that they will either pass or fail. They will therefore have to give the impression that they know the organizational script and are able to play it at least as well as, if not better than, the current performers (i.e. the selection panel). Too much assistance from the selectors will be seen as a sign of unfamiliarity and may lead to failure. That said, the selectors (i.e. the audience) have an integral and essential part to play. While they are the target of the performance they also have a role in its creation and realization. As Mangham (1986: 64) writes, 'Against this canvas, the social actors improvise their sallies, operating not out of a negotiated or exchange framework but out of a kind of theatrical intuition which enables each of them to know how to support or feed, whether by words or action, the others involved in the drama.' In other words, what the selectors are seeking is a certain 'natural' and spontaneous quality in the performance of the candidate, something that is complementary rather than too much at odds with their own performances and by definition the organizational script. This may be what many selectors refer to as having a 'gut reaction' about a particular candidate.

These performances are analogous to those given by a *Commedia dell' Arte* troupe. This was a school of performance that flourished in the sixteenth and seventeenth centuries in Italy and France. Mangham (1987: 13) writes that these 'Performers had in their command a large store of speeches and bits of "business" which they would exchange with their fellow players within a known framework. *Commedia* is an extempore art form played by professional actors, "off the cuff" (*a bracchia*) against a theme or a scenario (*canovaccio*)'. Each member of the troupe was assigned a specific, and different, character which remained the same regardless of the situation. Like Abbott and Costello, Laurel and Hardy, the Marx Brothers, Jerry Lewis or Norman Wisdom, whatever the plot or the situation in which they found themselves, they remained the same. The actors then improvised, within the same character, within a variety of situations. Therefore, what selectors are often looking for is a Bud Abbott to their Lou Costello or a Stan Laurel to their Oliver Hardy. The skill of the executive search consultant is to act as a sort of theatrical agent or impresario in identifying the part to be played and then finding the most appropriate person/actor to perform the role. The task, achieved through the candidates, is to produce a performance which resonates with the organizational script. Candidates have to convince the selectors that they are 'right' for the part; indeed, that the part was unknowingly and therefore unwittingly written for them. Executive search consultants manage this through a careful process of 'back-stage' selection, coaching, preparation and stage management. They conduct mock interviews, hold intensive briefings on the client organization and via detailed research into the candidate's career history determine the extent to which the client's requirements and the experience and future career aspirations of the candidate match.

Through these procedures they seek to assure themselves that they are putting someone forward who will perform well within the client's organizational setting. Wherever possible they seek to minimize the risk of the candidate rejecting a job offer or the client questioning the composition of the shortlist. Research evidence suggests that these are the two most common reasons for client dissatisfaction with executive search consultants.

A further important task for executive search consultants is to manage the inherent volatility and danger in the assignment process. Most of the danger attaches to the candidates: they are frequently of a level of seniority where their continuing public mastery of their senior roles would be seriously damaged if it were known that they had been rejected elsewhere. Poor reviews affect performers' confidence; they also affect the confidence of others around them. Given the fragile nature of senior executive reputation, public rejection would impact on their future capacity to carry off their roles with conviction. Hence, another essential feature of the headhunter role is to limit this danger.

Thus, in executive search activities the consultant manages the audition to minimize the risk to candidates, not simply by coaching and preparation but also in a sense by ensuring that the entire process remains back-stage – hidden. For those who fail the process, it never occurred – character and reputation remain intact. Their confidence, and that of those around them, will not be affected. Hence, a critical feature of the consultant role is 'the creation and management of impressions' (Mangham, 1978: 28). The executive search consultant's impression management is so total that there is no, or very little, public awareness of the event. The candidate's current employer, for example, is unaware of his or her participation in the recruitment process. Indeed, the process remains hidden from all except the active participants (candidates, consultant and client). Telephone calls and correspondence relating to the vacancy are commonly directed to the candidate's home. Meetings are often held after work or at the weekend.

In summary, when viewed in terms of the dramaturgical metaphor, executive search consultants can usefully be seen as impresarios, arranging and directing a certain sort of audition performance, managing impressions and limiting the dangers associated with 'risking character' – the candidates' and their own.

Management gurus

This section argues that management gurus achieve success and reputation by the nature and quality of their public performance. In developing this point it is helpful to ground an analysis of their activities in some illustration of what such consultants actually do. Fortunately there are examples of these activities that have been publicly displayed, such as the public performances of Tom Peters or the televised presentations of John Harvey-Jones. Peters is a particularly good example, and although, as with all successful consultants of this genre, his performance is unique and idiosyncratic, it nevertheless highlights a number of the key characteristics of such performances. According to Clark and Salaman (1995b), these include the following.

- A powerfully physical presentation with a great deal of restless energy.
- Demonic energy leading to near exhaustion.
- High levels of commitment and passion, which generate an intensity of experience for audience and presenter.
- Challenge, threat, confrontation. The audience is not allowed simply to sit and receive information (i.e. to spectate passively). It is brought into the event by challenge and attack.
- A Peters session is not going to be a bland, calm neutral presentation of options and possibilities; rather it is guided by conviction and certainty. The performer will show, *must* show, absolute certainty and conviction. If he falters, the audience falters. He must believe in himself so that the audience believes in him.
- The presence of danger, risk, surprise. It's not safe. The audience might be exposed, caught out at any moment. There will be threat and danger for all parties – presenter and audience alike. Things could go wrong. It might be embarrassing; in fact it almost certainly will. Anything may happen, but he will get away with it – but only just.
- The message is posed in riddles, in dilemmas, in mysteriously

gained insights that leave the 'audience' impressed by the performer's knowledge of them and their experience. The presenter 'knows' them, 'knows' their problems, 'knows' their subterfuges and tricks. They are open to the presenter and therefore susceptible to persuasion.

These are indicative of the central features of performances given by such consultants. Many of us have seen them. Indeed, some of us may have experienced them directly. They are extraordinarily powerful and impressive, and very different from the conventional 'dry' academic presentation of data, theory, conclusions, etc. Indeed, the appeal and popularity of these events is founded not on the empirical strength or content of the ideas being promulgated but on the way in which they are communicated. The important point to remember is that the dynamics of these events provide the performer with an opportunity to convince the management audience of his or her value and quality. This is inextricably linked to the main purpose of such events which is to convert the audience to the guru's way of thinking; to restructure managers' ways of thinking and in so doing to transform their consciousness. But how is this to be achieved? What are the specific features of these events that enable the guru performer to persuade and convert the members of the audience? In order to be able to answer this question fully it is first necessary to establish the aims of this type of consultancy work.

It is the contention of this book that the public performances of management gurus are exercises in persuasive communication. In essence these consultants are seeking to achieve transformations of consciousness in the audience members. According to Scheidel (1967: 57), the aim of persuasive speaking is to 'modify a listener's beliefs and/or affects toward the proposition advanced by the speaker'. He argues that persuasive speakers are seeking to change the attitudes, beliefs and value systems of audience members. These systems are the way in which we label, order and structure the complex and evolving world in which we live. However, they are not grounded in some kind of immutable truth since they have been invented not discovered. They 'exist in man rather than in nature' (Scheidel, 1967: 33). The boundaries and content of these categories may therefore change as we react to and evaluate different experiences. Therefore, an essential feature of our attitudes, beliefs and value systems is their potential vulnerability to external influences. As a consequence, they can be modified, shaped and moulded through the clever manipulation of certain persuasive techniques. This is echoed by Huczynski (1993: 245) who writes that 'A realistic aim of the guru's persuasive communication is not that his ideas should necessarily and immediately modify the *actions* of his audience, but that they should alter their *beliefs*, *attitudes* and *feelings* towards his suggestions.'

Why managers should be particularly vulnerable to the persuasive presentations of management gurus is a complex and, as yet, little understood phenomenon. However, in part it has something to do with the oral tradition in management. Gowler and Legge (1983: 198) have noted that management work consists largely of the spoken word and that organizational life involves two parallel orders of language: 'the rhetoric of bureaucratic control [which] conflates management as a moral order with management as a technical-scientific order, whilst submerging the former.' Similarly, Stewart (1976: 92) notes that 'management is a verbal world whose people are usually instructed, assisted and persuaded by personal contact rather than on paper.' In other words, managers are more influenced by verbal than by written communication.

A further reason for the susceptibility of managers to guru performances relates to the uncertainty created by the pressures for change outlined in the opening chapter of this book. This argued that the increasing use of management consultancies was the outcome of two interrelated factors: (a) environmental pressures forcing organizations to change; and (b) the new skills and qualities needed to manage new types of organization. These dual pressures are forcing managers to think in different ways. Managers are having to change by casting off inappropriate and/or redundant mind sets. These are being replaced by new skills and mind sets, which contain different success recipes. As a consequence, the categories that managers once found reassuring and relied on so heavily have been attacked, weakened, undermined and supplanted. Certainty has been replaced by uncertainty. Managers' cognitive categories are already being questioned. Management gurus offer certainty and a potential route through the complexities of modern management life.

How, then, do management gurus convert members of their audience to their way of thinking, and what mechanisms underlie their persuasive communication? Huczynski (1993: 243–67) has already considered these questions in some detail. Keeping in mind that the main purpose of guru performances is to achieve transformations of consciousness among the members of their management audience, he suggests that Lewin's (1951) three-phase model for creating, reinforcing and sustaining attitudinal change is the most appropriate framework for seeking answers to these questions. This model consists of three phases: unfreezing, changing and refreezing. The subsequent discussion, which relates the application of this model to the work of management gurus, draws on Huczynski's original analysis.

Unfreezing

This phase creates the conditions that are necessary if members of the audience are to change. It is a period in which the management guru seeks to 'soften up' the audience, to destabilize them, to make them indecisive, uncertain and self-questioning. In essence he or she seeks to disturb the taken-for-granted, unquestioned notions, mind sets and recipes that the members of the audience bring to the event. This depends on rousing strong emotions in their audience. According to Sargant (1976: 73), the management guru is more likely to be successful at achieving change if he or she 'can first induce some degree of nervous tension or stir up sufficient feelings of anger or anxiety to secure the person's undivided attention and possibly increase his suggestibility.' This is accomplished by increasing the emotional stress and heightening the level of expectations of the audience members. Management gurus seek to keep them on tenterhooks. They may use a variety of techniques to achieve this, such as delaying their entrance, 'milking' the applause as they enter the auditorium or displaying emotion and gratitude for the welcome. A point well made by Atkinson (1984: 18) is that when members of an audience applaud they are acting in unison. It is something that is done together. This has the effect of bringing the members of the audience together and begins their transition from attendees to active participants in the event. This is something that the guru will seek to build on and encourage throughout the duration of the performance. Through the creation of an emotionally charged atmosphere participants are more susceptible to threats and suggestion and less able to repel the assaults to their current ways of thinking.

Changing

Cleverley (1971: 102–6) has identified a number of reasons for managers changing their beliefs. Three are considered to be pertinent to the current discussion, since they are based on Firth's (1959, 1967) research into the conversion of the Polynesian island of Tikopia from a mostly pagan society into an almost completely Christian one. The first reason relates to the economic benefit. Managers hope that through their conversion their organization will become more successful: its economic performance will improve. Implementing the ideas propounded by the guru will unlock the currently restricted potential of their organization. Gurus reinforce this with constant references to organizations which have apparently succeeded by following their set of ideas. Oliver (1990: 20) recounts how, at a seminar conducted by Eli Goldratt, the co-author of *The Goal* (Goldratt and Cox, 1989), 'Goldratt introduced a large coloured gentleman to the audience . . . The gentleman introduced himself as Emerson, and then proceeded to describe what Goldratt's ideas had done for his company.' In a similar vein, other management gurus, such as Tom Peters or Rosabeth Moss Kanter, show videos or give examples of organizations which they claim to be exemplar cases for the ideas they are propounding. It is almost as if they are saying, 'Other people have done it and succeeded. Why don't you?'

Second, managers may be convinced that the idea is true. They may be persuaded by the empirical foundations of the ideas being promulgated. For instance, managers often attend a Peters or Kanter session clutching well thumbed and dog-eared copies of their books. They see the examples given by the guru, and, as mentioned above, sometimes hear first-hand testimony from those who have successfully followed the ideas being expounded by the guru. All these various sources of information contribute to an atmosphere in which no counterveiling or critical evidence is cited, thus giving the impression of the infallibility and desirability of adopting and implementing the guru's ideas.

Third, accepting the ideas provides the potential convert with some degree of comfort. As mentioned above, managers are facing and working with increased organizational change. They are seeking reassurance and support so that they can cope more effectively with the circumstances in which they find themselves. Cole's (1975) notion of the *illud tempus* is relevant here. Managers are seeking access to, or at least a glimpse of, some kind of management certainty in a world in which old certainties have been turned upside-down, made redundant and ineffective. They have to 'learn about, and possibly modify their management styles, or their team roles, they may need to learn about a new form corporate culture. They must learn to manage in ways which encourage innovation and participation and ensure quality. The message then is: learn, learn, learn' (Salaman and Butler, 1994: 35). The problem is that, as was noted in Chapter 5, managers are confronted with a bewildering array of alternative ideas. In contrast, management gurus represent certainty. This often comes from the experience of their own conversion. As Sargant (1976: 78) states with reference to the experience of John Wesley, 'Once habituated to the new pattern of thought, John Wesley set about implanting it in others.' Gurus therefore represent what managers most value: 'certainty, tied to prescription' (Salaman and Butler, 1994: 36).

In addition, Huczynski (1993: 257) suggests that management gurus achieve changes in managers' attitudes, beliefs and values through a combination of 'push-and-pull factors'. The major push factor concerns the encouragement of potential converts to identify with a new idea. Sargant (1976) suggests that this is achieved by contrasting the old and the new in such a way that the new is made more attractive. He writes, on the basis of studying the preaching style of John Wesley, that

one must also provide an escape from the induced mental stress. Hellfire is presented only as the result of *rejecting* the offer of eternal salvation won by faith. Emotionally disrupted by this threat, and then rescued from everlasting torment by a total change of heart, the convert is now in a state to be helped by dwelling upon the complementary gospel of Love.

(Sargant, 1976: 80)

Consultants similarly play on the uncertainty in managers' minds created by the initial onslaught to their taken-for-granted ways of thinking. They often juxtapose the 'old' and the 'new' in such a way that the 'new' undermines the 'old'. As a consequence managers feel less certain about and committed to their existing (i.e. 'old') and possibly cherished ways of thinking than before their attendance at the event. The 'new' offers a path towards certainty and apparent redemption, two goals sought by many managers. Those who may think of deviating and returning to 'old' recipes and ways of doing things, are aware that severe penalties may accompany their actions, since the contrast stresses the many deficiencies of the 'old'. Furthermore, conversion to the 'new' and rejection of the 'old' is often presented as a matter of extreme urgency. The ultimate scenario for failing to adopt the 'new' is organizational failure. This creates a sense of urgency, which increases the levels of anxiety and suggestibility among the audience members.

One example of this working in practice is given in Oliver's (1990) account of the Eli Goldratt seminar referred to earlier. At one point during this event he sought to draw out a contrast between the 'cost' and 'throughput' worlds. He then sought to show the key deficiencies of the 'cost' world and how these would become redundant once the 'throughput' world was embraced. Furthermore, one world was understood as 'bad' and the other as 'good'. He then attempted to show through a series of exercises that most of the managers in the room were entrenched in the 'bad cost' world and that 'It will not be easy to move from a cost world to the throughput world. We have to throw away much of what we have learnt over the last thirty years . . . We've met the enemy. It's us' (Oliver, 1990: 21).

Atkinson (1984: 73–82) suggests that this technique of 'contrastive pairs' is a common rhetorical technique, used by a wide variety of public speakers, that encourages the audience to be drawn into the process of their own persuasion. As a consequence the persuasive process becomes two-way. Instead of the persuader influencing the persuadee, gurus may create a context in which the managers in the audience contribute to their own persuasion. For instance, when confronted with these two-part contrasts managers are forced to make a choice and locate themselves in one or other of the categories. Are your ideas modern on the one hand or traditional and regressive on the other? Are you a follower or not? In this way gurus may claim that it was not they who convinced the audience members of the value of their ideas but the participants themselves. For example, when a member of the audience tells Goldratt, 'You've sold it to me,' he responds, 'No, you sold it to yourself' (Oliver, 1990: 25).

The pull factors relate to the 'release in tension which follows the acceptance of the new position; they value the comfort of having re-established their cognitive balance (after the unpleasant cognitive dissonance experience while being torn between the old and new views)' (Huczynski, 1993: 257). Having had their taken-for-granted mind sets battered, questioned and undermined, they find comfort in the new reassuring world being offered by the guru. Accepting the new leads to new-found confidence. Conversion ensures that the anxiety, indecision and self-questioning associated with the old way of thinking becomes a distant memory.

Refreezing

Having induced stress in the audience and thereby unfrozen them, eradicated, or at least led them to question, their previous ideas and offered new, more attractive and comfortable ones, the guru's next procedure is to reinforce and permanently to fix the change (Huczynski, 1993: 265). Lewin (1951) termed this refreezing, while Scheidel (1967: 76) referred to it as *resolving*, in which the focus is 'upon the fixing of the persuasive influence'. This occurs after the management guru's performance. Once the event has come to an end there is a danger that the audience members will revert to their old mind sets and ways of thinking. The actions of the guru that lead to changes in managers' ideas and categories occur during the persuasive speaking event. Once the guru performance is at an end and he or she has left the auditorium the receiving of information finishes and his or her persuasive influence diminishes. If the managers' attendance at the event is to have a long-lasting impact, the audience members must learn (i.e. internalize) some aspects of their restructured attitude, belief and value systems. Learning theory suggests that behaviour patterns which are rewarded tend to be repeated. As a consequence, a follow-up procedure is vital if recent converts are to remain steadfast in their commitment to their new-found beliefs. If this does not happen the speaker and the message will become separated, with the consequence that the guru's influence on their audience will dissipate. Gurus may attempt to overcome this by selling copies of videos of their performances, copies of their books and consultancy packages. In addition, they may ask participants to 'sign up to quality', or whatever idea the guru is expounding. Furthermore, in the case of the Goldratt seminar one recent convert announced the establishment of a TOC (theory of constraints) 'club'. This was to be divided into a number of chapters and participants were actively encouraged to join.

Therefore, management gurus, via the adoption and manipulation of a number of persuasive techniques, seek to reawaken, to generate fundamentally transformed 'consciousness' in their audience of self, management and organization, so that the audience members see new patterns and new possibilities that ordinary life, before the performance, had not made available or obvious. The focus is on the emotional and irrational, with all the fear and anxiety that this occasions for audience and performer. (And surely one's first impression on witnessing a guru performance is anxiety that the performance is so extravagant, so melodramatic, that it will appear absurd; but slowly this risk, being overcome by the performer, actually adds to his or her stature). But there is also risk for the audience. No one is safe. Those who hope that they can remain immune and detached as observers soon find that by a variety of devices they are drawn into the session, become the focus of the session, in which strange things happen to them. They may be exposed to combative questions, publicly posed with riddles, forced to reveal their ignorance, which is then immediately exposed, and required to participate in role plays. A battery of destabilizing techniques is used to move the content of the event from a safe, cerebral level to the level of 'here and now', with egos, identities and pride at stake, and with potentially significant alterations in status (e.g. senior manager to public incompetent). As Sargant (1976: 92) notes, the only way to remain unaffected is to stay away.

The focus of this type of performance is on the emotional, the generation of threat and risk for all parties, the destabilizing of identities, allied to the repetitive emphasis on simplified, action-focused, ritualistic nostrums, all presented in a style where confidence dominates over doubt, steadfastness over vacillation and optimism over pessimism, to create an environment where the consultants are able to generate a collective sense among the managers not only of power and impact, but also of truth and relevance. As Goffman (1990: 35) puts it (of performances), 'reality is being performed'.

Discussion of performance

While the usefulness of the work of Burke, Goffman and Mangham in detailing the structure of various kinds of perform-ance is noted, there is a need to move beyond their primarily theatrical conception of social intercourse, since theatrical acting is not the same as social acting. Hence, a guru performance is not the same as a theatrical performance. Rather, when we are considering the guru performance there is a need to enlarge the meaning of performance beyond its normal theatrical sense to include other sorts of performance, where the focus is less on the performer complying with a script for and to an audience, and more on the performer managing the whole event so that the audience actively contributes to and becomes involved in the creation of a performance. Thus, a guru performance does not refer to the sense of an occasion where individuals seek to present themselves to others in terms of certain roles (whether fixed, improvised, situational, personal or strategic), moods and atti-tudes, important as these are. A guru performance is not simply *role-play*, however interpreted. The view of performance being developed here owes more to Schechner (1977: 142) who writes: 'Performance originates in impulses to make things happen and to entertain; to get results and to fool around; to collect meanings and to pass the time; to be transformed into another and to celebrate oneself; to disappear and to show off.'

Schechner has developed this sense of performance in terms of five features: '(1) *process*, something happens *here and now*; (2) *consequential irremediable*, and *irrevocable* acts, exchanges, or situations; (3) *contest*, something is *at stake* for the performers and often for the spectators; (4) *initiation*, a *change in status* for participants; (5) space is used *concretely* and *organically*' (p. 51). While this definition captures accurately the intensity, power, danger and impact of the performances given by management gurus, there is a need to strengthen it by moving beyond this definition. These performances have the following additional features.

First, they depend on the 'performer', and on the performer's behaviour, not on other resources, bodies of knowledge, positions or accoutrements. The performer may create supportive accoutrement, out of everyday materials, but he or she does not depend on them. The relationship is the other way around: their role and importance is defined by the consultant's performance. In the same way, when a magician pulls something from a hat it does not matter whether it is a scarf, a bird, a dove or something else. The role of these props is to support and sustain the magician's actions, which comprise the overall performance. Similarly, a consultancy report, the candidate shortlist and the results from psychometric tests all have relevance in that they assist the consultant both to maintain and to realize a performance. Their relevance and role in the creation of the performance is orchestrated by the consultant. Care has to be taken when using materials and props since, as Mangham and Overington (1987: 102) write 'When attention focuses not upon the work in its entirety but upon the materials or techniques which have been used to create it, the frame is likely to break.' Put differently, once the audience's attention switches from the realization of the performance to the way in which it is put together the theatrical reality is undermined.

Second, a guru performance is not of the normal type, where

the performance is conceptualized as simply theatrical – as involving performers performing at, and to, a largely passive audience. In a theatrical performance the audience members retain a distance from what is enacted in front of them. They do so in the belief that the theatrical is 'an abstraction from the "blooming, buzzing confusion" of actuality' (Mangham and Overington, 1987: 103). Witnessing the murder of a character on stage does not cause anyone to call the police or for a doctor. In the guru performance the 'audience' is not the same as a theatre audience, it does not simply listen to and observe a representation of reality; rather, it is *central* to the performance itself. The audience is the *means* of the performance, its accomplice and its measurement. This conception of performance enlarges its meaning beyond its normal theatrical sense to include other sorts of performance, where the focus is less on the performer realizing a performance for an audience, and more on the 'performer' managing the whole event so that the audience has a positive experience. The latter relates both to the audience's experience of participation and to the outcome resulting from the interaction. To achieve this the performance is created, adapted and realized so as to meet the needs of a particular audience. Yet without the consultant the audience members are unable personally to re-create the event. As in the theatre, once the curtain is down and the actors have left the stage, the audience is helpless. It is reduced to a loose assembly of individuals who were once active participants in the realization of a theatrical event. They may want more, and indicate this by shouting vociferously at the end of a performance, but without the actors on stage they are unable to re-create the event in which they have just participated.

Third, and building on the previous point, the duration of a guru performance depends upon the actions of the performer. It ends when he or she brings it to a close. Once he or she disconnects from the audience the performance is over. The interaction, and therefore the event, is at an end. The audience members are left with memories and impressions of an experience from which they may attempt imperfect and partial recreations. Yet without the central catalyst (i.e. the performer) there is no performance. As a consequence, a performance perishes once the final curtain calls are taken and the performer leaves the stage. However, as suggested above, the message he or she seeks to convey may be reinforced with the sale of books, videos and consultancy packages.

Fourth, a guru performance is highly risky, and may go disastrously wrong. It involves the manipulation of techniques and materials of an unusual kind, and in an unusual way.

Fifth, the performance generates remarkable tension, excitement and energy, which cannot be ascertained simply from an account of the event or from its formal content (or from those sad and often empty souvenirs – off-prints, copies, handouts), but has to be 'experienced' directly. It is thus highly dependent on the individual consultant.

Sixth, the event deals in emotion. Regardless of the cognitive content of the performance, the power and effects of the performance *qua* performance are inherent in the emotion it generates and displays, and therefore success occurs as much (if not more) on the emotional level as on the rational, cognitive level. Emotion can at best be described to others but cannot be experienced indirectly. As Goffman (1990: 35) puts it, 'there is an expressive rejuvenation and reaffirmation of the moral values of the community.'

Seventh, the event is characterized by mystery, by riddle, the world turned upside down, paradox, amazement, surprise and threat. Consciousness, expectation and normality are turned upside down. Status is at risk, identities can be undermined, relationships questioned and convictions unsettled.

In summary, when examined in terms of the dramaturgical metaphor the work of management gurus can be seen as a particular type of public performance. Their performances are exercises in persuasive communication. By employing particular techniques of persuasive communication, management gurus seek to convert their audience of managers to their way of thinking. They seek to achieve transformations of consciousness in audience members. However, while these performances share many features with theatrical performances they are not the same. These performances cannot be construed as strictly theatrical. The guru performance is less concerned with making a script real, or 'present', for a passive audience, and more focused on the active management of the whole event so that the audience contributes to and becomes involved in its own process of conversion. As a consequence, a guru performance is dependent upon the actions of the performer; the audience is central to the creation and realization of the performance; and it lasts for as long as the performer is 'on stage'.

Conclusion

The argument has been presented and the supporting evidence marshalled. In a sense the performance that encompasses this book is at an end. It is therefore time to turn from performer to critic and reflect on what has been presented. This gives an opportunity to draw the various threads together so that the reader is able to understand how the two specialist case studies discussed in this chapter seek to supply answers to and illuminate the issues discussed earlier in the book, relating to market features, service characteristics, reputation, dramaturgical metaphor, etc. Although the text has been realized for the audience, in this case for you the reader, there is still a need to examine the linkages between each scene so that the central themes of the performance become more clearly known. What follows can be likened to a director's commentary after a film has been shown. This enables members of the audience to perhaps see certain nuances they may have missed and understand the creator's intentions behind what was presented to them on the screen.

In essence, this book has sought to identify the main problems associated with using management consultancies and how these are overcome. It began by arguing that the current pressures for organizational change and the qualities required to manage the new 'learning' organizations have created a context in which managers are increasingly turning to management consultancies for assistance with designing and implementing organizational change programmes. As a result the management consultancy industry has been one of the most vibrant and successful parts of the British economy during the 1980s. It grew by a little over 200 per cent between 1985 and 1992.

This apparently unfettered growth seems curious given that

the use of management consultants is inherently problematic. In particular, clients are faced with two key problems: (a) ascertaining the quality of a supplier of management consultancy services prior to purchase; and (b) evaluating the quality of the service once it has been delivered. These problems are particularly acute given the nature of the management consultancy market and service.

Low barriers to entry have underpinned the recent rapid expansion of the industry. Entry is in effect 'free'. This situation has two important implications for clients. First, they have a wide range of suppliers from which to choose. Second, the lack of any structural barriers to entry has meant that clients are responsible for distinguishing between high and low quality consultancies prior to contracting with a particular supplier. However, determining the relative quality of consultancies is made difficult by a number of service characteristics. In particular, intangibility implies that a service does not take on a physical form. Ascertaining the quality and relevance of a service prior to purchase is therefore problematic. Indeed, intangibility may imply that clients view consultancies as perfectly substitutable, since they are unable to determine the relative quality of the alternatives they may be considering. Furthermore, the characteristic of interaction suggests that there is nothing to evaluate until the client and consultant meet to produce the service. As a consequence, service production is inherently social. This underpins the heterogeneity of services, since the centrality of client–consultant interaction ensures that no two assignments will be the same. Each service purchase is therefore unique, implying that past performance may not be repeated in the future. When seeking to purchase a management consultancy service, a client must therefore seek to overcome these endemic problems.

Given these problems the book has sought to answer two key questions: (a) how do clients choose suppliers of management consultancy services; and (b) how do consultants manage the interaction process between clients and consultants in such a way that they convince clients of their value and quality?

In answer to the first question the book has sought to argue that clients choose suppliers of management consultancy services primarily on the basis of institutional (i.e. a consultancy's) and personal (i.e. a consultant's) reputation. Reputation refers to clients' *perceptions* of suppliers' service quality based on their evaluation of services delivered in past periods. In other words, reputation refers to those conceptions, 'images' or understandings that clients have of suppliers' services. These 'images' are generally derived from two sources: (a) direct experience of a particular supplier (first-hand reputation); and (b) recommendation from valued and trustworthy informants (third-party reputation). In both instances reputation is something that is *created* via the process of interaction. It is a dynamic process in which buyers use assessments of their past experiences with suppliers as a way of forecasting future quality. In other words, buyers use their experience of interacting with suppliers to determine whether they are likely to deliver a high or low quality service. On the basis of these evaluations clients decide whether to use the same supplier at some point in the future or recommend them to others. Reputation is therefore socially constructed over time. It is dependent upon the quality of client–consultant interaction. If consultants are to be successful and convince clients of their quality and worth a core feature of their work must be to manage the way in which these 'images' of their service quality are formed. Since these evaluations are based upon a client's experience of the interaction process it is natural that this will be where consultants' impression management activities will be concentrated. In this sense the art of persuasion is at the core of management consultancy work.

Having established that impression management is a core feature of consultancy work, the book sought to answer the second question: how do consultants convince clients of their value? What is it that they do that conveys to clients the 'image' of a high quality service? This question was approached by examining the work of consultants in terms of the dramaturgical metaphor. This metaphor is useful since it focuses on the most important feature of consultancy work – the interaction process. It is concerned with highlighting what happens when social actors, in this case clients and consultants, meet and 'work' together. Furthermore, at the heart of this metaphor is a concern for the creation of meaning and management of impressions. Existing metaphorical conceptions of consultancy have failed to recognize this central aspect of consultancy work. On the basis of Goffman's and Mangham's conception of the social actor this book has sought to emphasize the way in which consultants seek actively to manipulate the interaction process (i.e. the consultancy script) by bringing into play their personal and strategic scripts and so ensuring that these create a tailored image of their service. Consultants are able to do this as a result of the intangibility of the management consultancy service. This implies that clients are unable to discern the nature of the service they have purchased until it has been produced. Up to that point it lacks a material form; in effect it does not exist, it only has potential, it remains an unkept promise. This implies that clients do not know what they are getting until they get it. They 'get it' by interacting with the consultant. Once the service has been produced clients then have something, primarily their experiences of the interaction process, which they can then use in order to evaluate the quality of the service they have received. This situation permits consultants to create and construct a reality, by managing the interaction process, which persuades clients that they have received a high quality service delivered by experts. Furthermore, the heterogeneity of services enables consultants to tailor the delivery of their service to the particular needs of their clients.

The book then sought to apply the dramaturgical metaphor to two types of consultancy activity – executive search and management guru performances – in order to demonstrate the way in which this metaphor highlights how consultants seek to build their personal reputations by creating and managing impressions of the service they deliver via their interaction with clients. At first it may appear that the choice of these two examples is a little peculiar since they are not usually considered mainstream consultancy activities. Furthermore, they are very different from each other. Why, therefore, were they chosen? These case examples were selected because they represent very different types of consultancy activity and are therefore able to test the general appropriateness of the dramaturgical metaphor to the work of consultants. At the same time, the differences and contrasts between these two types of consultancy work emphasize different aspects of the metaphor.

Thus, executive search is seen as a 'back-stage' activity in which the interaction process with clients is managed indirectly. Consultants seek to create impressions of their service by carefully managing the meeting between the client and candidates. This arises since clients evaluate the value of an executive search service in terms of the quality of the candidates presented to them. Executive search consultants therefore have two key tasks. The first is to identify candidates whom they believe to be right for the part (i.e. the vacancy). Second, they must prepare each candidate so that his or her 'appearance', 'manner' and performance resonate with that demanded by the organizational script. Through careful and supportive coaching, directing, rehearsal and stage management the executive search consultant prepares each candidate for the 'first night'. At the audition (i.e. the selection interview) each candidate is then able to convey and demonstrate mastery of the organization he or she is striving to join. At the same time, by ensuring that the whole assignment processes remains covert, consultants manage the risk which attaches to candidates if they should fail. For those who fail it never happened. In summary, examining the activities of executive search consultants in terms of the dramaturgical metaphor suggests that they convince clients of their value and quality through the careful selection and preparation of candidates prior to the selection interview. The candidates are then able to present themselves in terms of the characters and roles demanded by the client organization. The quality of an executive recruitment service is therefore determined by the quality of the shortlist presented to the client.

In contrast, when viewed in terms of the dramaturgical metaphor the work of management gurus is more explicitly theatrical. It is a 'front-stage' activity in which they seek, through emotionally charged public performances, to achieve transformations of consciousness in their audience of managers. They achieve this by exploiting a number of persuasive techniques (e.g. 'contrastive pairs') that take their audience through a sequence of phases – unfreezing, change, refreezing – in order to create, reinforce and sustain attitudinal change. Such a focus is not only the key to understanding this type of consultancy work – it is also the key to the consultant's success. Successful management gurus have always known, and exploited, what was outlined earlier in the chapter: that success and reputation depend on the magic and mystery of the performance. Given the constraints and characteristics of the consultancy industry the management and achievement of an impressive public performance is the only possible way in which they are able to convince clients of their value and quality. Hence, these public performances are central to both the effectiveness of the consultant and to his or her competitive success within the industry.

NOTES

1 Introduction

1 These were identified through a technique known as the 'closed loop' method. Several hundred consultancies were initially identified through their entries in a number of relevant industry directories. As a precursor to the questionnaire survey each of these consultancies was contacted for a list of their competitors. This was repeated with each newly identified consultancy until a closed loop was achieved (that is, no new consultancies were identified). The questionnaire was then sent to all 841 consultancies thus identified.

2 The management consultancy market

1 The results from these studies are summarized in Table 4.1.
2 As will be shown in Chapter 4, this track-record does not necessarily have to relate to the management consultancy industry. Where the requirements for providing a good quality service are similar between services, reputation may be transferred between these services.
3 This is developed more fully in Chapter 5.
4 While these data are limited to just 60 consultancies, the findings reflect earlier research conducted by Keeble *et al.* (1990: 22) into the entry of 869 management consultancies between 1950 and 1990.

4 Choosing a management consultant

1 The licence fee has remained the same since the provisions of the Act came into force in 1976.
2 The converse may also be true; lapses in quality in one market may destroy the reputation a firm has nurtured in other markets.

5 The dramaturgical metaphor

1 Mangham (1978) argues that the role of the consultant is precisely to help managers uncover the scripted nature of their performances and to expose mutually hidden back-stage areas.
2 A Shaman is a religious figure whose distinctive activity is going into a trance. Hungan is a Haitian term for the priest of a possession cult.

BIBLIOGRAPHY

Abbott, P. (1995) Survey: Andersen tops the league in a growing market, *Management Consultancy*, July/August, 16–29.
Accountancy (1993) News, *Accountancy*, July, 13–14.
Akerlof, G.A. (1970) The market for 'lemons': qualitative uncertainty and the market mechanism, *Quarterly Journal of Economics*, 84, 488–500.

Alchian, A.A. and Woodward, S. (1988) The firm is dead; long live the firm: a review of Oliver E. Williamson's 'The Economic Institution of Capitalism', *Journal of Economic Literature*, 26, 65–79.

Alvesson, M. (1993) Organisations as rhetoric: knowledge-intensive firms and the struggle with ambiguity. *Journal of Management Studies*, 30, 997–1015.

Alvesson, M. (1994) Talking in organizations: managing identity and impressions in an advertising agency, *Organization Studies*, 15, 535–63.

Arndt, J. (1979) Toward a concept of domesticated markets, *Journal of Marketing*, 43, 69–75.

Ashridge Management Research Group (1987) *Management for the Future*. Berkhampstead: Ashridge Management Research Group/Foundation for Management Education.

Askvik, S. (1992) Choosing consultants for OD assignments, paper presented to the International Organization Development Association World Conference, University of Coventry, November.

Atkinson, M. (1984) *Our Masters' Voices*. London: Methuen.

Bain, J.S. (1956) *Barriers to New Competition*. Cambridge, MA: Harvard University Press.

Bain, J.S. (1968) *Industrial Organization* 2nd edn. New York: John Wiley.

Batstone, S.J. (1991) New business service firms: an exploratory study, in L.G. Davies and A.A. Gibb (eds) *Recent Research in Entrepreneurship*. Aldershot: Avebury.

Beatty, R.P. and Ritter, J.R. (1986) Investment banking, reputation, and underpricing of initial public offerings, *Journal of Financial Economics*, 15, 213–32.

Beer, M., Eisenstat, R.A. and Spector, B. (1990) Why change programs don't produce change, *Harvard Business Review*, November/December, 158–66.

Beer, M., Eisenstat, R. and Spector, B. (1988) *The Critical Path to Change: Developing the Competitive Organization*. Boston, MA: Harvard Business School Press.

Beesley, M.E. and Hamilton, R.T. (1984) Small firms seedbed role and the concept of turbulence, *Journal of Industrial Economics*, 33, 217–31.

Belkaoui, A. and Pavlik, E. (1991) Asset management performance and reputation building for large US firms, *British Journal of Management*, 2, 231–8.

Bevan, A. (1974) The UK potato crisp industry, 1960–72: a study of new competition, *Journal of Industrial Economics*, 22, 281–97.

Blake, R.R. and Mouton, J.S. (1983) *Consultation: a Handbook for Individual and Organizational Development*. Reading, MA: Addison-Wesley.

Bibliography

Blau, J. (1984) *Architects and Firms*. Cambridge, MA: MIT Press.

Block, P. (1981) *Flawless Consulting: a Guide to Getting Your Expertise Used*. Austin, TX: Learning Concepts.

Bloomfield, B.P. and Best, A. (1992) Management consultants: systems development, power and the translation of problems, *Sociological Review*, 40, 533–60.

Bloomfield, B.P. and Danieli, A. (1995) The role of management consultants in the development of information technology: the indissoluble nature of socio-political and technical skills, *Journal of Management Studies*, 32, 23–46.

Bryson, J., Keeble, D. and Wood, P. (1993) The creation, location and growth of small business service firms in the United Kingdom, *Service Industries Journal*, 13, 118–31.

Buchanan, D. and Boddy, D. (1992) *The Expertise of the Change Agent: Public Performance and Backstage Activity*. London: Prentice Hall.

Burke, K. (1945) *A Grammar of Motives*. Berkeley: University of California Press.

Burke, K. (1969) Dramatism, in *International Encyclopedia of the Social Sciences*, Volume VII. New York: Macmillan.

Burns, T. (1992) *Erving Goffman*. London: Routledge.

Business Statistics Office (1985) *Size Analysis of United Kingdom Businesses, 1985 (PA 1003)*. London: HMSO.

Business Statistics Office (1992) *Size Analysis of United Kingdom Businesses, 1992 (PA 1003)*. London: HMSO.

Byrne, J.A. (1986) Business fads: what's in – and out, *Business Week*, January, 40–7.

Callon, M. (1986) Some elements of a sociology of translation: domestication of the scallops and the fishermen of St Brieuc Bay, in J. Law (ed.) *Power, Action and Belief*. London: Routledge and Kegan Paul.

Clark, I. and Clark, T. (1990) Personnel management and the use of executive recruitment consultancies, *Human Resource Management Journal*, 1, 46–62.

Clark, T. (1993a) *Headhunters of Enterprise: Executive Search and Selection Consultancies*. Small Business Research Trust Business Services Research Monograph No. 1, School of Management, Milton Keynes: The Open University.

Clark, T. (1993b) The market provision of management services, information asymmetries and service quality – some market solutions. An empirical example. *British Journal of Management*, 4, 235–51.

Clark, T. and Mabey, C. (1994) The changing use of executive recruitment consultancies by client companies, 1989–1993, *Journal of General Management*, 20, 42–54.

Clark, T.A.R. and Salaman, G. (1993) The use of metaphor in the client–consultant relationship: a study of management consultants, paper delivered to Conference on Professions and Management in Britain, University of Stirling, August.

Clark, T.A.R. and Salaman, G. (1994) Understanding consultancy as a performance: the dramaturgical metaphor, paper delivered to Conference on Metaphors in Organizational Theory and Behaviour, Kings College London, July.

Clark, T. and Salaman, G. (1995a) Understanding consultancy as performance: the dramaturgical metaphor, in I. Glover and M. Hughes (eds) *Professions at Bay*. Aldershot: Gower.

Clark, T. and Salaman, G. (1995b) The use of metaphor in the client–consultant relationship, in C. Oswick and D. Grant (eds) *Organizational Development: Metaphorical Explorations*. London: Pitman.

Clark, T. and Salaman, G. (1995c) Management gurus as organizational witch doctors, Open University Business School Working Paper Series No. 3.

Clarke, R. (1985) *Industrial Economics*. Oxford: Blackwell.

Cleverley, G. (1971) *Managers and Magic*. London: Longman.

Cole, D. (1975) *The Theatrical Event: a Mythos, a Vocabulary, a Perspective*. Middleton, CT: Wesleyan University Press.

Coleman, J.S. (1988) Social capital in the creation of human capital, *American Journal of Sociology*, 94 (supplement), S95–S120.

Coulson-Thomas, C.J. (1991) Developing tomorrow's professionals today, *Journal of European Industrial Training*, 15, 3–11.

Czarniawska-Joerges, B. (1990) Merchants of meaning: managing consulting in the Swedish public sector, in B. Turner (ed.) *Organizational Symbolism*. New York: de Gruyter, 139–50.

Dale, M. (1994) Learning organizations, in C. Mabey and P. Iles (eds) *Managing Learning*. London: Routledge.

Daniels, P.W., Leyshon, A. and Thrift, N.J. (1988) Large accountancy firms in the UK: operational adaptation and spatial development, *Service Industries Journal*, 8, 315–46.

Dawes, P.C., Dowling, G.R. and Patterson, P.G. (1992) Criteria used to select management consultants, *Industrial Marketing Management*, 21, 187–93.

Dietrich, M. and Holmes, P. (1991) Financial institutions and the estate agents industry in the 1980s, *Service Industries Journal*, 11(4), 481–90.

Drucker, P. (1988) The coming of the new organization, *Harvard Business Review*, January–February, 45–53.

Dumaine, B. (1989) What the leaders of tomorrow see, *Fortune*, 3 July, 24–34.

Bibliography

Dwyer, R.F., Schurr, P.H. and Oh, S. (1987) Developing buyer–seller relationships, *Journal of Marketing*, 51, 11–27.

Evely, R. and Little, I.M.D. (1960) *Concentration in British Industry*. Cambridge: Cambridge University Press.

Firth, R.W. (1959) *Social Change in Tikopia: Re-study of a Polynesian Community after a Generation*. London: Allen & Unwin.

Firth, R.W. (1967) *Tikopia: Ritual and Belief*. London: Allen & Unwin.

Flipo, J.-P. (1988) On the intangibility of services, *Service Industries Journal*, 8, 286–98.

Franklin, P.J. and Woodhead, C. (1980) *The UK Life Assurance Industry: a Study in Applied Economics*. London: Croom Helm.

Ganesh, S.R. (1978) Organizational consultants: a comparison of styles, *Human Relations*, 31, 1–28.

Gill, J. and Whittle, S. (1992) Management by panacea, *Journal of Management Studies*, 30, 281–95.

Goffman, E. (1990) *The Presentation of Self in Everyday Life*. Harmondsworth: Penguin.

Goldratt, E.M. and Cox, J. (1989) *The Goal*. Aldershot: Gower.

Goold, M. and Campbell, A. (1987) *Strategies and Styles: the Role of the Centre in Managing Diversified Corporations*. Oxford: Blackwell.

Gowler, D. and Legge, K. (1983) The meaning of management and the management of meaning, in M. Earl (ed.) *Perspectives on Management*. Oxford: Oxford University Press.

Granovetter, M. (1985) Economic action and social structure: the problem of embeddedness, *American Journal of Sociology*, 91, 481–510.

Granovetter, M. (1992) Problems of explanation in economic sociology, in N. Nohria and R.G. Eccles (eds) *Networks and Organizations: Structure, Form and Action*. Boston, MA: Harvard Business School Press.

Greenfield, H.I. (1966) *Manpower and the Growth of Producer Services*. New York: Columbia University Press.

Greiner, L.E. and Metzger, R.O. (1983) *Consulting to Management*. Englewood Cliffs, NJ: Prentice-Hall.

Hales, C.P. (1986) What do managers do? A critical review of the evidence, *Journal of Management Studies*, 23, 88–115.

Hill, C.W.L. and Pickering, J.F. (1986) Divisionalization, decentralization and performance of large UK companies, *Journal of Management Studies*, 23, 26–50.

Hines, H.H. (1957) Effectiveness of 'entry' by already established firms, *Quarterly Journal of Economics*, 7, 132–50.

Höfl, H. and Linstead, S. (1993) Passion and performance: suffering and the carrying of organisational roles, in S. Fineman (ed.) *Emotion in Organizations*. London: Sage.

Managing consultants

Hoggett Bowers (1987) *A Career in the City – a Survey of High Earners*. Leeds: Hoggett Bowers.

Holmstrom, B. (1985) The provision of services in a market economy, in R.P. Inman (ed.) *Managing the Service Economy: Prospects and Problems*. Cambridge: Cambridge University Press.

Howells, J. and Green, A.E. (1986) Location, technology and industrial organisation in UK services, *Progress in Planning*, 26, 83–184.

Huczynski, A.A. (1993) *Management Gurus: What Makes Them and How to Become One*. London: Routledge.

Jackall, R. (1988) *Moral Mazes: the World of Corporate Managers*. Oxford: Oxford University Press.

Jenkins, I. (1970) Performance, in R.D. Smith (ed.) *Aesthetic Concepts and Education*. Chicago: University of Illinois Press.

Kanter, R.M. (1989) The new managerial work, *Harvard Business Review*, November–December, 85–92.

Keeble, D., Bryson, J. and Wood, P. (1990) Small firms, business service growth and regional development in the UK: some empirical findings. Small Business Research Centre Working Paper No. 7, University of Cambridge.

Keeble, D., Bryson, J. and Wood, P. (1994) *Pathfinders of Enterprise: the Creation, Growth and Dynamics of Small Management Consultancies in Britain*. Small Business Research Trust Business Services Research Monograph No. 3, School of Management, The Open University, Milton Keynes.

Klein, B. and Leffler, K.B. (1981) The role of market forces in assuring contractual performance. *Journal of Political Economy*, 89, 615–41.

Kubr, M. (1986) *Management Consulting: a Guide to the Profession*, (2nd edn), Geneva: International Labour Office.

Kuhn, T.S. (1970) *The Structure of Scientific Revolutions*, (2nd edn). Chicago: University of Chicago Press.

Lakoff, G. and Johnson, M. (1980) *Metaphors We Live By*. Chicago: University of Chicago Press.

Latour, B. (1987) *Science in Action: How to Follow Scientists and Engineers through Society*. Cambridge, MA: Harvard University Press.

Law, J. (1992) Notes on the theory of the actor network: ordering, strategy and heterogeneity, *Systems Practice*, 5, 379–93.

Legge, K. (1994) On knowledge, business consultants and the selling of TQM, unpublished paper, Lancaster School of Management, University of Lancaster.

Levitt, T. (1981) Marketing intangible products and product intangibles, *Harvard Business Review*, 59, 94–102.

Levitt, T. (1983) *The Marketing Imagination*. New York: Free Press.

Lewin, K. (1951) *Field Theory in Social Science*. New York: Harper Collins.

142

Bibliography

Lippitt, G. and Lippitt, R. (1979) *The Consulting Process in Action*. La Jolla, CA: University Associates.

Lyman, S.M. and Scott, M.B. (1975) *The Drama of Social Reality*. New York: Oxford University Press.

Macneil, I.R. (1980) *The New Social Contract: an Inquiry into Modern Contractual Relations*. New Haven, CT: Yale University Press.

Maister, D.H. (1989) Marketing to existing clients, *Journal of Management Consulting*, 5, 25–32.

Makridakis, S. (1992) Management in the twenty-first century, in D. Mercer (ed.) *Managing the External Environment*. London: Sage.

Management Consultancies Association (1994) *Management Consultancies Association*. London: Management Consultancies Association.

Mangham, I.L. (1978) *Interactions and Interventions in Organizations*. Chichester: John Wiley.

Mangham, I.L. (1986) *Power and Performance in Organizations*. Oxford: Blackwell.

Mangham, I.L. (1987) A matter of context, in I.L. Mangham (ed.) *Organization Analysis and Development*. Chichester: Wiley.

Mangham, I.L. (1990) Managing as a performing art, *British Journal of Management*, 1, 105–15.

Mangham, I.L. and Overington, M.A. (1983) Dramatism and the theatrical metaphor, in Morgan, G. (ed.) *Beyond Method*. London: Sage.

Mangham, I.L. and Overington, M.A. (1987) *Organizations as Theatre: a Social Psychology of Dramatic Appearances*. Chichester: Wiley.

Mann, H.M. (1966) Seller concentration, barriers to entry and rates of return in thirty industries, 1950–1960, *Review of Economics and Statistics*, 48, 292–307.

Margulies, N. and Raia, A. (1972) *Organization Development: Values, Processes and Technology*. New York: McGraw-Hill.

Megginson, D. and Pedler, M. (1992) *Self-development: a Facilitator's Guide*. Maidenhead: McGraw-Hill.

Mills, D.Q. and Friesen, B. (1992) The learning organization, *European Management Journal*, 10, 146–56.

Mills, P.K. and Margulies, N. (1980) Toward a core typology of service organisations, *Academy of Management Review*, 5, 255–65.

Mintzberg, H. (1980) *The Nature of Managerial Work*. New York: Prentice Hall.

Mitchell, V.W. (1994) Problems and risks in the purchasing of consultancy services, *Services Industries Journal*, 14, 315–39.

Morgan, G. (1980) Paradigms, metaphors, and puzzle solving in organization theory, *Administrative Science Quarterly*, 25, 605–22.

Morgan, G. (1983) More on metaphor: why we cannot control tropes in administrative science, *Administrative Science Quarterly*, 28, 601–7.

Morgan, G. (1986) *Images of Organization*. London: Sage.

Morgan, G. (1992) Proactive management, in D. Mercer (ed.) *Managing the External Environment*. London: Sage.

Nayyar, P.R. (1990) Information asymmetries: a source of competitive advantage for diversified firms, *Strategic Management Journal*, 11, 513–19.

Nees, D.B. and Greiner, L.E. (1985) Seeing behind the look-alike management consultants, *Organization Dynamics*, Winter, 68–79.

Nelson, P. (1970) Information and consumer behaviour, *Journal of Political Economy*, 78, 311–29.

Oakley, K. (1993) Management consultancy – profession or knowledge industry?, paper presented to Conference on Professions and Management in Britain, University of Stirling, August.

Oberoi, U. and Hales, C. (1990) Assessing the quality of the conference hotel service product: towards an empirically based model, *Service Industries Journal*, 10, 700–21.

O'Farrell, P.N. and Hitchens, D.M. (1990) Producer services and regional development: key conceptual issues of taxonomy and quality measurement, *Regional Studies*, 24, 163–71.

O'Farrell, P.N., Hitchens, D.M. and Moffat, L.A.R. (1993) Competitive advantage of business service firms: a matched pairs analysis of the relationship between generic strategy and performance, *Service Industries Journal*, 13, 40–64.

O'Farrell, P.N. and Moffat, L.A.R. (1991) An interaction model of business production and consumption, *British Journal of Management*, 2, 205–21.

Oliver, N. (1990) Just-in-time: the new religion of Western manufacturing, Paper presented to British Academy of Management Conference, Glasgow, September.

Ortony, A. (1975) Why metaphors are necessary and not just nice, *Educational Theory*, 25, 45–53.

Ortony, A. (1979) *Metaphor and Thought*. Cambridge: Cambridge University Press.

Pascale, R.T. (1991) *Managing on the Edge*. Harmondsworth: Penguin.

Pedler, M., Burgoyne, J. and Boydell, T. (1986) *A Manager's Guide to Self-development*. New York: McGraw-Hill.

Peet, J. (1988) A survey of management consultancy: outside looking in, *The Economist*, 13 February, 1–19.

Pepper, S.C. (1942) *World Hypotheses*. Berkeley, CA: University of California.

Perinbanayagam, R.S. (1974) The definition of the situational: an analysis of the ethnomethodological and dramaturgical view. *Sociology Quarterly*, 15, 521–41.

Bibliography

Pettigrew, A. and Whipp, R. (1991) *Managing for Competitive Success.* Oxford: Blackwell.

Purcell, J. and Ahlstrand, B. (1994) *Human Resource Management in the Multi-divisional Company.* Oxford: Oxford University Press.

Rashid, S. (1988) Quality in contestable markets: a historical problem, *Quarterly Journal of Economics*, 103, 245–9.

Rathwell, J.M. (1974) *Marketing in the Service Sector.* Cambridge, MA: Winthrop.

Salaman, G. (1995) *Managing.* Buckingham: Open University Press.

Salaman, G. and Butler, J. (1994) Why managers won't learn, in C. Mabey and P. Iles (eds) *Managing Learning.* London: Routledge.

Sargant, W. (1976) *Battle for the Mind.* London: Heinemann.

Sashkin, M. and Burke, W.W. (1990) Organization development in the 1980s and an end-of-the-eighties retrospective, in F. Masarik (ed.) *Advances in Organization Development.* Norwood, NJ: Ablex.

Saunders, K.C. (1991) Service without a smile: the changing structure of the death industry, *Service Industries Journal*, 11, 202–18.

Schank, R.C. and Abelson, R.P. (1977) *Scripts, Plans, Goals and Understanding.* Hillsdale, NJ: Laurence Erlbaum.

Schechner, R. (1977) *Performance Theory.* New York: Routledge.

Scheidel, T.M. (1967) *Persuasive Speaking.* Glenview, IL: Scott, Foresman.

Schein, E.H. (1969) *Process Consultation: Its Role in Organizations' Development.* Reading, MA: Addison-Wesley.

Schlegelmilch, B.B., Diamantopoulos, A. and Moore, S.A. (1992) The market for management consulting in Britain: an analysis of supply and demand, *Management Decisions*, 30, 46–54.

Schön, D. (1979) Generative metaphor: a perspective on problem-solving in social policy, in A. Ortony, A. (ed.) *Metaphor and Thought.* Cambridge: Cambridge University Press.

Schroder, H.M. (1989) *Managerial Competence: the Key to Excellence.* Iowa: Kendall/Hunt.

Sears, H. (1982) Use of consultants for senior appointments, unpublished MBA dissertation, Cranfield University.

Senge, P. (1990) The leader's new work: building learning organizations, *Sloan Management Review*, 32, 7–23.

Shapiro, C. (1983) Premiums for high quality products as returns to reputations, *Quarterly Journal of Economics*, 43, 659–79.

Sheldon, R.R. (1966) *Viktor Shklovsky: Literary Theory and Practice, 1914–1930.* Ann Arbor: University of Michigan Press.

Shostak, G.L. (1977) Breaking free from product marketing, *Journal of Marketing*, 41, 73–80.

Sinha, D.P. (1979) *Consultants and Consulting Styles.* Delhi: Vision Books.

Starbuck, W.H. (1992) Learning by knowledge-intensive firms, *Journal of Management Studies*, 29, 713–40.

Steele, F. (1975) *Consulting for Organizational Change*. Amhurst, MA: University of Massachusetts.

Stewart, R. (1976) *Contrasts in Management*. London: McGraw-Hill.

Stock, J.R. and Zinszer, P.H. (1987) The industrial purchase decision for professional services, *Journal of Business Research*, 15, 1–16.

Storey, J. and Sisson, K. (1993) *Managing Human Resources and Industrial Relations*. Buckingham: Open University Press.

Syrett, M. (1988) Management consultants: time for a check-up?, *Director*, April, 82–6.

Thomson, A., Pettigrew, A. and Rubashow, N. (1985) British management and strategic change. *European Management Journal*, 3, 165–73.

Tilles, S. (1961) Understanding the consultant's role, *Harvard Business Review*, November–December, 87–99.

Tisdall, P. (1982) *Agents of Change: the Development and Practice of Management Consultancy*. London: Heinemann.

Turner, B. (1990) The rise of organisational symbolism, in J. Hasard and D. Pym (eds) *The Theory and Philosophy of Organisations*. London: Routledge.

Underwood, L. (1989) Management consultants look for world power, *Director*, June, 131–9.

Walker, R.A. (1985) Is there a service economy? The changing capitalist division of labour, *Science and Society*, 49, 42–83.

Watson, H., Ball, D., Britton, C. and Clark, T. (1990) *Executive Search and the European Recruitment Market*. London: The Economist Publications Limited.

Whitely, R. (1989) On the nature of managerial tasks and skills: their distinguishing characteristics and organization, *Journal of Management Studies*, 26, 209–24.

Williamson, O.E. (1975) *Markets and Hierarchies: Analysis and Antitrust Implications*. New York: Free Press.

Wilson, A. (1972) *The Marketing of Professional Services*. London: McGraw-Hill.

Wood, S. (1986) Personnel management and recruitment, *Personnel Review*, 15, 3–11.

Woodworth, W. and Nelson, R. (1979) Witch doctors, messianics, sorcerers, and OD consultants: parallels and paradigms, *Organizational Dynamics*, Autumn, 17–33.

INDEX

Index

reading, 105
realization of, 105–6
restaurant, 114
situational, 103, 104, 107, 108, 126
strategic, 103, 104–5, 107, 108, 109, 126
Sears, H., 111
Senge, P., 6, 7
services
  characteristics, *see*
    heterogeneity; intangibility;
    interaction; perishability
  evaluation of, 12–14
  implications of, 57–63
  types of service organization, 46–7
shaman, 106, 137
Shapiro, C., 75
Shostak, G.L., 43
Sinha, D.P., 89
Sisson, K., 2
social capital, 80
Starbuck, W.H., 60
Steele, F., 88
Stewart, R., 119
Stock, J.R., 28, 70
Storey, J., 2
Syrett, M., 27

T value, *see* turbulence

Thomson, A., 2
Tikopia, 121
Tilles, S., 88
Tisdall, P., 24
Touche Ross, 27
transformations of consciousness, *see* managers
turbulence, 34–7, 38, 39, 40, 71, 72
Turner, B., 92
two part contrasts, 123–4

Underwood, L., 34
unfreezing, 120–1
Urwick, Orr and Partners, 22, 23, 27

VAT, 23

Walker, R.A., 42
Watson, H., 77
Wesley, J., 122
Whipp, R., 4
Whiteley, R., 90
Whittle, S., 90
Williamson, O.E., 77
Wood, S., 113
Woodward, S., 54, 63
World Hypotheses, 95

Zinszer, P.H., 28, 70